TEACHING YOUR CHILD BASIC BODY CONFIDENCE

Patty Carmichael Gerard
with Marian Cohn

Photographs by Meryl Joseph

Houghton Mifflin Company
Boston   1988

Acknowledgments

I would like to acknowledge the many people who have made this book possible: I am especially indebted to the children who have participated in my classes, without whom I could not have developed my program; my parents, Dr. and Mrs. Paul Carmichael, and my sister and brothers, particularly Paul Jr. and Joe; a special acknowledgment to my dear friends, Mary McCabe, Mary Ann Engel, Tamara Pawlichka and Patrick Hannon.

Special thanks to all of the delightful children who appear in the photographs: Danielle Avedon, Jennifer Avedon, Tanisha Blake, Adam Brodsky, Ben Casper, Jessica Casper, Matthew Delaney, Ariel Eisenberg, Jesse Eisenberg, Greta Fails, Ryan Feury, Christina Gerard, Lily Gold, Nathan Goldman, Amanda Harris, Amanda Knappman, Jonathan Kreisky, Zoë Larson, David Lipton, Natalie Van der Meer, Peter Sohr, Lucy Caron Stein.

Text copyright © 1988 by Patty Carmichael Gerard Illustrations © 1988 by Lynn Sonberg Book Services

All rights reserved.

For information about permission to reproduce selections from this book, write to Permissions, Houghton Mifflin Company, 2 Park Street, Boston, Massachusetts 02108.

Book design by Sonja Douglas

Published by arrangement with Lynn Sonberg Book Services 166 East 56 Street New York, NY 10022

The clothing worn by many of the children in this book was generously contributed by Hanna Andersson, a direct-mail children's clothing importer located at 1010 N.W. Flanders, Portland, Oregon 97209. (800-222-0544). The equipment used was contributed by American Athletic Corporation, Cedar Rapids, Iowa.

Printed in the United States of America

M 10 9 8 7 6 5 4 3 2 1

Library of Congress Cataloging-in-Publication Data

Gerard, Patty Carmichael.
  Teaching your child basic body confidence / Patty Carmichael Gerard with Marian Cohn.
     p.   cm.
  Includes index.
  ISBN 0-395-44253-2. ISBN 0-395-47590-2 (pbk.)
  1. Child development.   2. Motor learning.
3. Movement education. 4. Self-confidence in children.   I. Cohn, Marian.   II. Title.
RJ133.G47   1988   87-29796
649'.57—dc19   CIP

This book is dedicated to my greatest blessing,
my beautiful daughter, Christina "Critter" Gerard.
She reignited my love of learning,
inspired me through her joy of discovery and
infused me with hope for the future.

CONTENTS

1
WHY YOU NEED THIS BOOK

Remember when you looked at your newborn infant and realized for the first time how completely he or she depended on you for survival? A lifetime's worth of hopes and dreams for your child's future was probably born in that moment. Perhaps you've noticed yourself watching older kids in a playground and wondering what your baby will be like when he matures. Will he be agile and fearless like the girl who climbs to the top of the jungle gym without a second's hesitation? Will he be outgoing and sociable like the boy in the sandbox who always seems to attract a circle of playmates? Or will he be withdrawn and shy like the toddler who sits on the sidelines and watches in bewilderment the ease with which the others play and climb?

As a mother myself, I know the only thing that seems certain to a new parent is that the helpless tot in your arms will enter this social world soon enough. He will be walking, talking, running and jumping—capable of getting into all sorts of challenging situations without you there to prompt or help or oversee. If you are like me, surely you want your child to have the skills and self-assurance that are the basic tools for success in life.

Yet you may not have any idea of how to foster the transition from total reliance to self-sufficiency. Perhaps you assume that nature simply takes its course.

It is true that all normal, healthy children naturally learn to walk, run and jump. However, not all children learn to walk, run and jump *correctly*. Mobility is so basic to life that we tend to take its development for granted; we tend to believe the elementary motor skills evolve on their own, given enough time. Yet look at any group of adults for proof that physical competence does not always develop automatically.

Is physical competence really all that important to your child's start in life? The answer, according to specialists in child development, is an overwhelming yes. In the early years, a child's intellectual and psychological growth is intimately connected to his ability to move and physically explore the environment. The process of learning about the world begins with sensory-motor experience. It is a child's first way of knowing and understanding.

Some researchers go as far as to say that a child's self-concept is largely related to how he sees himself physically. Watch a group of children play. They recognize and admire one another's agility or strength long before they recognize which one is the smartest.

Specialists have long recognized that all youngsters develop motor skills at varying rates but in the same sequence. And new scientific evidence indicates that learning takes place most readily during certain growth periods, and that the failure to master basic skills in a step-by-step progression at these optimum times will affect all subsequent skill development. In other words, when learning is delayed beyond the critical phase, the skill is more difficult—or even impossible—to learn well. Unfortunately, left on their own, children do not always master the full range of skills needed for thorough development.

As a world-class gymnast and professional coach, I was especially concerned that my own child get a good foundation in physical and motor skills early in life. When Christy, my daughter, was born in 1981, I wanted sound information about how to evaluate her motor progress, how to recognize key periods for learning, and how to promote thorough skill mastery. To my surprise, I found that no scientific, systematic program of skill building existed. I decided to create my own, using the latest research in child development and human performance summed up in the Body Color Theory.

The Body Color Theory describes all human movement in terms of three imaginary color-coded axes that run through the body. It explains why motor skills develop in a particular sequence and how this learning progression actually structures and promotes mental development. The Gerard Method combines the Body Color Theory principles of progressive skill learning with safe and sound coaching techniques derived from my own athletic training into a program of creative play techniques for parents to practice with infants and young children. The "color" of movement makes the Gerard Method easy to follow and fun to do.

Of course, the ability to acquire skills also depends on genetically determined factors. Physical maturity—body size, neuromuscular development, etc.—has an influence on a child's readiness. However, creating timely and appropriate opportunities for learning is equally important. A child who has reached the critical period for crawling, for example, cannot develop the skill well if he is cooped up in a playpen day after day. The Gerard Method teaches you *when* and *how* to intervene to enhance the natural process of skill development in order to ensure that learning is timely and complete.

I believe that thorough is best—not that sooner is better. The Gerard Method relies on nature to set the pace, so you avoid pressuring or stressing your child. While there is scientific evidence to show that delayed skill learning may be harmful, there is no research to support the notion that early skill development is advantageous.

The Gerard Method offers an easy way to turn your daily play time with your youngster into truly quality time, strengthening bonding, language and motor skills while you and your child are having fun. In only fifteen to thirty-five minutes a week, this comprehensive program will help your child develop the basic skills and self-confidence that will serve him for a lifetime.

2
THE COLOR OF MOVEMENT

The Body Color Theory, which is the scientific basis of the Gerard Method, grew out of my research for National Aeronautics and Space Administration scientists. It is the first comprehensive theory to define the progressive development of movement at every level of human performance. It explains both how infants learn to walk on earth and how astronauts learn to "walk" in space. You don't need to understand the theory to use the Gerard Method successfully, but this chapter is provided for those who would like more background information.

The Body Color Theory, simply stated, defines all human performance in terms of three fundamental components—force, space and time—each of which has a specific correlation to the axes of movement. To grasp the specific relationships of force, space and time to high-level human performance, you need to know complex formulas. Fortunately, however, to understand how I use the Body Color Theory in this book does not require much more than a little imagination.

The "colors" of movement are actually simple and fun to learn. Once you know them, you can easily recognize the colors in almost every motor activity. The un-

derlying premise of the Body Color Theory is that all movement takes place on one of three imaginary axes. The theory gets its name from the fact that each axis is given a color to identify it:
• The blue axis runs up and down through the body from head to toe.
• The yellow axis passes through the body from front to back.
• The red axis goes through the body from side to side.
It is important to remember that axes remain in the positions described above whether the body is upright, upside down or sideways.

You can move *along* or *around* each of these three axes. Try these simple exercises for yourself to see how moving on your axes feels. (You can actually perform these movements or just imagine them.)
• Stand still, then grab an imaginary axis and pull yourself along it. When you pull along blue, you should feel yourself move up and down as if you're jumping. When you pull along yellow, you should feel yourself moving forward or backward, depending on the direction you pull. When you pull along red, you should feel

yourself sidestepping from left to right or right to left. In gymnastics, these movements are called translations on the axes.

• Now, stand still, grab an imaginary axis and *turn it* in either direction, as if that axis were the axle running through the hub of a wheel. Then *imagine* (*don't* attempt to perform these movements unless you are a gymnast!) your body is attached to that wheel axle, and feel your entire body move around it in the direction it is turning. In gymnastics, these exercises are called rotations on the axes. If you rotate on blue, you should feel yourself slowly rotating like a top. If you turn on yellow, you should feel yourself moving as if performing a cartwheel. If you rotate on red, you should feel your body moving in a forward or backward roll, depending on the direction of the rotation.

What color is your body? We say it's blue when you move on blue, yellow when you move on yellow, and red when you move on red.

If you have imagined yourself moving along and around each colored axis, then you have just visualized the full range of potential motion. Even the highly complex skills performed by Olympic gymnasts are simply variations or combinations of these basic movements on the axes.

The colors are so simple to learn, yet their application to movement theory has produced important new insights. When I started using the Body Color Theory in my work with children, scientists had already identified the learning progressions of those motor skills considered to be "inherently human"—rolling over, crawling, pulling to a stand, walking, jumping, walking sideways—

AXES OF MOVEMENT

Translation: Movement along an axis

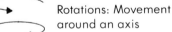

Rotations: Movement around an axis

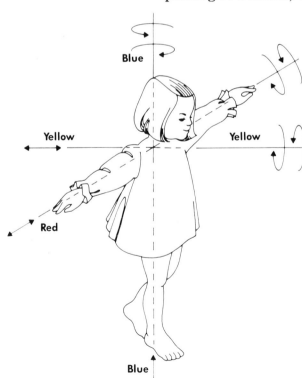

but they had little insight into *why* skills developed in this way. Beginning with the known progressions, I applied the colors to the various skills to see if the theory would yield any new understanding about the development of movement. A definite pattern emerged.

I saw that all motor development could be divided into stages related to specific body axes. For example, rolling over, crawling and pulling to a stand, achieved in the first year of life, are all blue axis movements. Mastery of blue axis movement is demonstrated by the ability to maintain balance while standing—that is, the ability to "be blue." Balancing on blue is the basis for bipedal motion, the next stage of motor development: walking and running, or the ability to move along yellow; jumping in place, or the ability to move along blue; and walking sideways, or the ability to move along red, which toddlers master between the ages of 1 and 2½ years. The ability to move along, or translate, on all three axes is prerequisite to the third stage of motor development, between the ages of 2½ and 6, when youngsters learn to rotate on red and yellow, master "flight-phase" skills and also learn to combine colors for the first time.

Movements combine colors when the body moves along or around one colored axis but *through* a different-colored space. Space has planes of color just as the body does. The planes of space are fixed by the force of gravity. The color of space is determined by the direction of the body's motion through it: movements that go up and down define blue space; movements that go forward or backward define yellow space; and movements that go left or right define red space.

For example, imagine you are walking along your yellow axis; then imagine that the axis extends beyond your body into space, so space is yellow, too. Now imagine extending the axis of movement into space as you jump up and down on blue or sidestep on red. In each case, body and space color remain consistent. But what happens if you hop forward? Your body moves up along the blue axis at the same time it moves forward through yellow space. The movement *combines* colors. This ability is essential to high-level skills.

In the earliest stage of motor growth, from birth to 1 year, body color is blue whether the infant is rolling over, crawling or pulling to a stand. However, there is no space color. At this age, an infant's sense of himself as separate from the world is growing, but the larger environment is still experienced as one undifferentiated "not me." As yet, the infant, confined to the ground, has no spatial awareness or sense of direction. He is only experimenting with force in movement, testing his own strength against gravity. We could say, from the point of view of the infant, that the body is blue, so the world is blue—but the concept of space as something with dimensions apart from himself does not exist.

LEVEL ONE: BIRTH TO 1 YEAR

MOVEMENT	BODY COLOR
Rolling over	Blue
Crawling	Blue
Pulling to a stand	Blue

At the next stage of growth, from 1 to 2½ years, a child learns to move on two feet along all three axes, and as he does, he explores space for the first time. He discovers a sense of direction—up and down, right and left, front and back—as a function of the force of gravity and his upright posture. Whether he walks, sidesteps or jumps, his body axes are aligned with the planes of space. At this stage of development, body and space color are always consistent, a characteristic unique to "inherently human" motor skills.

LEVEL TWO: 1 TO 2½ YEARS

MOVEMENT	BODY COLOR	SPACE COLOR
Walking	Yellow	Yellow
Running	Yellow	Yellow
Stepping sideways	Red	Red
Jumping in place	Blue	Blue

Not until the third stage of development, when the child learns to hop, skip, turn and spin ("flight-phase" and rotational skills), does the body move on different axes through all colors of space. These skills, which manipulate the body's relationship to gravity and space, are not "inherently human." Normal, healthy children naturally learn to walk and run simply by watching others, but most youngsters must be taught how to turn and spin, and they learn these skills through great effort.

The high-level motor skills, in which colors are combined, require more highly developed, integrated brain functioning.

LEVEL THREE: 2½ TO 6 YEARS

MOVEMENT	BODY COLOR	SPACE COLOR
Forward roll	Red	Yellow
Cartwheel	Yellow	Red
Hop forward	Blue	Yellow
Jump sideways	Blue	Red

Actually, the concept of body axes is not new to scientists, who commonly refer to them as the x, y, and z axes. What's new about the Body Color Theory is the analysis of skill development in terms of the axes—and, of course, the idea of color-coding them. What's in the name? The colors make the axes easy to visualize. Besides, kids love the idea because the colors make skill learning into a game. Parents love them because the colors are a simple teaching tool that makes skill learning easy and fun.

You can introduce the concept of the colored axes to your youngster at the age of 2½ or 3. (In chapter 7, the game called What's My Color? offers simple tips on how to do this.) As you progress through the challenging exercises in the last level of the program, you'll find that the colors help your child follow directions, relate different skills and master activities more easily.

3
WORKING WITH YOUR CHILD

The coaching tips in this chapter are based on techniques I originally developed for teaching my daughter, Christy. I wanted a program for her that was safe and sound. As a highly trained athlete in a sport where even a small error can cause crippling or fatal injury, I knew the importance of a scientific, systematic approach to developing physical skills. Yet I discovered that no program on the market met my standards for thoroughness and safety.

Applying principles based on my professional training and on solid child development research, I devised my own system to coach Christy through the natural process of physical and motor growth. Later, I expanded this system into a step-by-step program to teach skills to children of all ages. The teaching and coaching techniques I created for Christy are an integral part of the Gerard Method program. Their purpose is to give you the confidence and know-how to create a fun, safe, and effective environment for learning.

As you read through this chapter on coaching, keep in mind that each new skill is a discovery for your child. Every day he is learning new ways to move through space and adapt to gravity. Your role is simply to act as a guide to this young explorer. You can clear the path, provide opportunities for movement, point out pitfalls and even hold his hand along the way, but always let your child set the pace of progress. If you pressure your child, you will take the spontaneity and pleasure out of an experience that should be natural and fun.

This chapter is *your* guide to working with your child. It explains how to recognize when he has reached a key period for learning; how to coach him through a skill using proven techniques; how to encourage skill development without pushing; how to handle spills and falls and minimize your child's fears; how to evaluate your child's progress; how to foster positive attitudes toward challenge and competition and at the same time make skill learning exciting.

Knowing when your child is ready to learn
Give a kid a brand-new toy. He looks at it curiously, puts it down and, within seconds, it's forgotten. For weeks, your most imaginative efforts fail to entice him to pay it more attention, until one day you discover him playing

with the toy in total fascination—and nothing you do succeeds in getting his attention away!

What happened?

Your child has hit a key learning period. All of a sudden there is something about that object or activity that is stimulating your youngster's brain, and he seems to need it like food. He can't get enough of it! What you are witnessing is one of the most profound aspects of human development, and it's your cue to jump in and lend nature a hand to ensure that skill learning is correct and complete.

The Gerard Method is designed to capitalize on these crucial periods when kids are most ready to learn. When you turn to the program in Part Two, you will see that the activities are arranged in a special sequence. Since this order is the same for all children, you don't have to guess which activity your child is ready to tackle next, but as his coach, you do have to determine *when* your child is ready to try it and *how* to introduce each new activity when the time is right.

When a certain child is ready depends on several variables. A child cannot learn a new skill unless his neuromuscular system is mature enough to handle it. No matter how many times you stand a 4-month-old on his feet, he won't be able to hold himself upright until his body and nervous system can handle it.

A child's size and build also affect the pace of development, as well as the types of skills in which he may excel. For instance, toddlers who are likely to grow taller than average tend to have larger heads than their shorter peers. Because of this extra weight, taller kids may learn balancing skills slightly later than average.

Genetics plays a determining role in how fast and big a child grows. However, physical development is affected by environmental influences, too. Poor diet, dis-

ease and injury may delay maturity, while good health, proper diet and exposure to opportunities for learning may enhance growth.

While early skill development has not been proven beneficial, research does indicate that skills are more difficult—or even impossible—to learn *well* when learning is delayed beyond a key period. Your job is to provide your child with the appropriate learning opportunity at the optimal time for learning. The secret to recognizing when that time has arrived is simple: your child will let you know by a spontaneous show of interest and attention.

This doesn't mean you must never try an activity with a child before he discovers it for himself. On the contrary, in order for skill learning to be successful, two events must coincide: opportunities for learning must be present at the same time your child is ready to learn. Your job as coach is to provide these opportunities when you can.

Setting up a time and place

Setting aside specific times of day for acquiring skills allows children the chance to exercise and burn up excess energy and gives parents an opportunity to monitor motor development. Of course, the physical contact and fun naturally strengthens bonding, too. Before you begin any planned activity, be sure the environment is conducive to learning:

• Children learn best in a safe, relaxed atmosphere. A quiet, open area where you and your child can play undisturbed by others and free from the distraction of television or a clutter of toys is ideal. Be sure the room is well lit and well padded or carpeted, and always check all furniture, toys and equipment for unsafe or broken parts before using them. (Most of the equipment needed for the activities in this program are things you can find around the house, such as rattles, balls, stuffed toys, pillows, books and blocks, or special setups you can make out of household items.)

• Be sure your child is comfortable, too. Infants thrive on physical contact, so, as long as the room is warm enough, no clothes at all are just fine on the baby fitness scene. For older children, loose-fitting (not baggy) clothes or leotards are preferred. Unless otherwise instructed, bare feet are always best for learning, particularly for balancing and gross motor activities.

• Create the proper frame of mind. The psychological environment is just as important to skill learning as the physical. Children learn best when they are rested and alert but not rambunctious—perhaps in the morning or after a nap or a bath, and at least one hour after any meal. Avoid exercising when a child has just been very active or when he is sleepy, cranky, hungry or wet. No matter how carefully you have inspected a room or prepared for play, skill learning will be neither safe nor relaxed for a child who is distracted or fatigued.

• Never spend more than 60 seconds on a "lesson"—and only 20 seconds with newborns and small babies—until your child expresses his interest for more. This is one of the most important principles of the program. As long as you follow it, you will avoid pushing your child.

Your child's own readiness is the most important aspect of his learning environment, and whenever, wherever he takes an interest in learning, that is the time to provide the opportunity, encouragement, and supervision he needs to continue his exploration safely. Many times you will discover your child spontaneously testing out some new motor skill in the middle of his ordinary routine. Indeed, for infants and toddlers, discovering what the body can do *is* the ordinary routine! Don't stop

him because the physical environment isn't ideal. Just be sure to clear away any sharp or dangerous objects in the immediate area, and coach your child according to the usual guidelines.

The best moment for learning is unique for each child, but you will soon tune in to the right time for your own. By the way, don't try new activities unless you are ready, too. When you are tired, irritable or distressed, Junior is sure to feel it, and all the best coaching techniques in the world will not turn halfhearted efforts into a positive learning experience.

Choosing the right activity

The 96 activities in the program are arranged in sequence, from birth through 72 months, according to the average age at which each skill is learned.

The right activity for your child is the skill that is most appropriate to his level of maturity. Since all children develop skills in the same progression, the key to choosing the right activity is simply to determine which skill your child learned last and then to proceed to the next one in the program.

Obviously, if your child is a newborn, start the program with the first activity, and when he has learned that one, go forward in order. If, for example, your child is 8 months old when you begin the program, turn to the 6-to-9-month activities in Level One. Read through the goals in order, and start the program with the first activity your child cannot yet do.

Remember:

• Never introduce any skill unless your child has already learned the prerequisites for that activity. As long as your child can do the required skills, you can introduce an activity—regardless of his age.

• If you start the program in the middle, read through

the activities from the beginning to be sure that your child has not skipped any steps in his development. If he has missed a skill, go back and do it.

• Select two or three activities from different skill areas to work on at the same time. Motor development occurs within five distinct areas of skill—balance, strength, coordination, gross motor and fine motor—and you will see that all activities, beginning at 12 months of age, are categorized according to type of skill. These different areas develop concurrently, so your child may learn to walk on a floor beam, swing on a bar, bat a ball and jump, for instance, all within the same span of time.

• It may take many weeks between the time you introduce a skill and the time your child finally learns it. To allow for learning time, skills that are learned at an average age of 6 months, for example, will be listed in the "3 to 6 Months" section, not the "6 to 9 Months" section.

Demonstrating the skill

In the Gerard Method, skill learning for toddlers over 12 months begins with a two-part demonstration of the activity. Demonstrations are useless during the early months of life, since newborns cannot even differentiate between parts of their *own* bodies, no less between their own movements and yours.

• Give a visual demonstration by performing the skill yourself or using a doll. The demonstration should always be done when you have your child's complete attention. Do it as slowly as possible without losing the "look" of the movement, so your child realizes that effort is required to perform the skill.

• Don't demonstrate the skill perfectly the first time. Present it at a level of competency comparable to your youngster's. For instance, when you show your child how

to walk along a floor beam, you should look more like a wobbling clown than a seasoned tightrope walker in a high wire act. Improve your performance as your child's skill improves.

• Give a physical demonstration of the activity by carefully moving your child's body according to the written directions. In the early stages of growth, you will move your child's body through the skills as you might move a doll. However, as his muscle control and strength grow, your child will feel less like a puppet in your hands. Then, you will not so much move his body through the skill as physically support his attempts to do it.

Eventually, your child will learn to perform the skill through a process of matching his actual attempts at the movement to his mental image and "muscle memory." This matching process is a method of problem solving that can be applied to all new activities, and children learn it naturally when skills are introduced in a systematic manner, starting with the demonstration.

Giving instructions and encouragement

Children are inexperienced, but they are not dumb. In fact, they are remarkably direct and perceptive creatures—far more so than we adults sometimes give them credit for.

I once saw a young gymnast perform a routine on the mats as her coach looked on. When she was finished, the coach launched into a critique of her performance, using words like *angle, speed, force* and *trajectory*. The girl listened patiently for several minutes, then suddenly interrupted. "Sir, could you please just tell me," she said, "did I jump too soon or too late?"

When you're directing your child through a skill, keep your comments simple and brief. Key words and short phrases interjected at appropriate points will make learning easier, faster and more successful. Even infants will listen with pleasure to the sound of your voice, and while they may not understand all of the words, the constant communication from you will stimulate language development.

Here are some general tips on what to say and when to say it:

• Before you start, have your child focus on a specific object. Focusing is important because it settles a child's attention, eliminates distractions and narrows down the visual data necessary for performing a skill. In addition, focusing improves concentration, which is vital to safety. Finally, focusing teaches a child where to look as he moves—a lesson that seems unnecessary only if you have not yet been traumatized by the sight of your toddler running forward while devotedly looking back at you!

Be sure to give your child something pleasing to focus on; his favorite toy or colorful stickers usually do the trick. Whatever you use, the object should be placed approximately four feet away, or at a distance close enough to the child so that he can easily see it but far enough away so that he doesn't have to drop his head to look—and thereby upset his balance.

Some young children may not be too receptive to focusing. If that is the case with your toddler, don't make an issue of it. Tell him where to look once or twice and then go on.

Newborns, of course, cannot focus on anything that is more than a few inches from their nose. Fortunately, however, for their own survival they are programmed to focus on a human face, and especially on the eyes. So just be sure to have your baby's attention on you when starting an activity.

• Say "Ready!" when your child starts a skill and "Okay!" or "Very good!" when he completes it. Kids don't neces-

sarily understand when an activity begins and ends unless you let them know. For instance, the child learning to jump for the first time will often show by the look of excitement on his face that he believes he has accomplished the goal, although all he has managed to do was bend and extend his knees in an unsuccessful attempt to mimic you. Having never been off the ground independently before, he has no way of knowing whether he has achieved the "flight phase" of the jump.

Without a clear start and finish, children cannot recognize the learning process in between, and afterward they cannot adequately evaluate what they've accomplished in order to improve it next time.

• Always announce the name of the skill. When your child has focused and assumed the starting position for a skill, give a one- or two-word instruction. Say "Christy, jump!" or "Tommy, hop backward!"—whatever phrase gets the message across most succinctly. Children will commit an activity to memory more quickly when they associate a word with it.

• Whenever your child completes a skill, make one positive comment and one constructive comment only. I cannot overemphasize the need to support and encourage your child's efforts. As coach, you must present challenges in a positive way, always focusing on your child's successes and keeping your comments balanced, clear and brief.

First, pick one positive aspect of your child's performance, *no matter how trivial,* and praise it. If he just fell off the beam, tell him how well he got up and stood on the beam to start with. Then offer a short comment—*not* a criticism—on how to make the skill better. If he fell off the beam three times before he got to the end, then suggest that next time he can aim for the end of the beam in two tries.

It's inevitable that your child will not do the skill correctly on the first try; *no* child ever does. Still, he may feel that he did a wonderful job, as in the case of the jumper above. After all, he *felt* his body moving up and down, just as yours appeared to do in the demonstration. This is a sensitive moment. If you have a disappointed look on your face, or if you say "No, no!" and redemonstrate, you may undermine his self-confidence and willingness to try the activity again—and, possibly, future ones as well.

On the other hand, once he becomes proficient, it is important not to overpraise his efforts, either. Your child should leave the session feeling self-satisfied yet challenged, knowing he can improve his performance the next time he tries.

Spotting

Spotting, or physically holding and assisting a youngster through an activity, is a skill in itself. As a parent, you are probably spotting your toddler all the time, by balancing him as he sits on your lap or holding him upright as he first attempts to stand. But sometimes your spontaneous efforts to assist may unintentionally hinder rather than help by interfering with your child's vision, balance or control.

In this second step of skill learning, your child *actively* initiates a new activity while you spot his attempts. As the spotter, you must know how to handle your child's body without getting in the way of the movement or giving the wrong "feel" or "look" to it. Remember, the goal of spotting is to give your child the right information about how to control a skill so he eventually learns to do it on his own.

Each activity in the program includes specific, step-by-step, illustrated instructions on how to assist safely and effectively. However, there are some general rules on spotting that apply to all skills (unless otherwise instructed):

• Never stand directly in front of your child. Stand beside or behind him so he has a clear view of the space in which the skill will be executed. Vision is important to performance and safety. If you're spotting right in front of him—especially if he's a toddler—he may cry when you move away because he is used to seeing you there in order to do the skill. You've "taught" him that your visual presence is part of the activity!

• Never hold your child's hands above shoulder level. When a young child stands or walks on his own, his natural balancing point is slightly above the waist. If you raise his arms much above that point when spotting, you will shift his center of balance, altering the skill altogether. Lacking a correct sense of balance, he will not be able to control his movements on his own.

• Always maintain your spotting position. When you see your child perform a skill by himself for the first time, this is *not* a cue to move away. Mastering a skill takes time, and for safety's sake, you should always be ready to assist.

• Reverse the instructions for right and left if your child is not "right-side dominant." Since 90 percent of the population prefers to use the right hand and right foot for motor activities, the spotting instructions are written for right-handed children.

Note that a child can be right-side dominant in many skills yet prefer his left side to perform "power skills" like kicking or batting. If you don't know your child's dominant side, here's a way to find out. Stand directly in front of your child—not off to either side—and offer him a toy to hold. The hand he naturally uses is his preferred hand. For your toddler, put a foam ball directly in front of and between his feet and ask him to kick it. The foot he uses is his preferred foot.

Mastering skills

The goal of skill learning is independence and self-control. In this final stage of the three-step process, your coaching participation is mostly through demonstrations and verbal assistance. Continue to spot your child as instructed, but allow him to initiate the skill, following his attempts closely and giving hands-on help only when necessary.

Once the basic skills are mastered, they are mastered for life. For the purposes of the program, there's no value in practicing accomplished skills over and over, unless it's just for fun. The object is to give your child a good grasp of the basics. Whether he can run far or jump high is insignificant, as long as he can run and jump *well*. As a general rule, a child has mastered an activity when he can do it on his own in eight out of ten tries over the course of hours or days—*not* eight times in a row.

Remember, physical competence and self-confidence result from building skills systematically—and this holds true for individual exercises as well as for skill development overall. The goal is not to accomplish the hardest skills quickly but to develop good control each step of the way and then go on to the next level.

Handling tumbles, tears and fears

The step-by-step approach of the Gerard Method promotes safety and reduces risks of accident and injury, but a flop here and there is unavoidable as your child goes through the natural process of trial and error that is part of learning.

While you cannot prevent every tumble and fall, you can act to minimize the fear of falling, which in the long run can do far more damage to your child's confidence and ability than an occasional bump or bruise.

• As much as possible, do not overreact when your child falls. Here's a scenario I'm sure you've seen at the playground. Little Johnny is playing happily and suddenly falls down. Looking stunned, perhaps, but no worse for wear, he starts to get up by himself. All of a sudden, Daddy rushes over and, as if on cue, Johnny bursts into tears.

Children tend to get frightened in response to their parents' fright, which causes them to doubt their own feelings. If you gasp or show alarm, your child may believe that something is wrong or that what he's doing is unsafe—and he will cry out of fright, not injury.

Be careful not to condition this response in your child. Help him to understand that crying should be reserved for true injury only. Help him learn to listen to his own body and trust the information it gives him. When he's really hurt, he will let you know, and when he starts crying on his own, of course go over to help him immediately.

• When he does fall, have your child repeat the skill right away. Help him recognize that learning is a process of trial and error. When he takes a spill, stand him right up and show him what he can do to avoid his error next time. For example, if he tripped on an edge, have him tap his toe against it so he sees how that action will block his safe passage. Then help him repeat the activity correctly.

• Be an alert coach. Your toddler is not in grave danger of getting hurt as long as you properly childproof the play area and remain ready to assist him. Coaching and safety go hand in hand. The better you do your job, the safer and more secure your child will be.

Measuring your child's progress

My daughter is not as flexible or as fast as other kids because she is short. Christy knows she cannot run as quickly as her friend down the block, but she takes great pride in her strength, which is exceptional for her age, and her talent in this area gives her a sense of security and worth.

I believe that measurement and competition can be helpful tools to development if properly used, not as a way to challenge others but as a challenge to improve oneself. Each challenge successfully completed builds a child's self-confidence and self-esteem.

Measurement is an important part of a coach's job. It's meaningless to say that a child is either good or bad at movement; however, it may be useful to know that she is better in some skills than in others. By keeping track of those areas in which your child excels and those in which her skills are lacking, you can give extra help to suit her needs and ensure that her development is well rounded.

If you would like to systematically monitor your child's progress throughout the course of the program, you can plot her "learning curve" on the evaluation graphs in chapter 8. Or you can just spot check as she completes each activity by mentally comparing your child's age with the "average age learned."

Be aware, however, that this average is *not* the goal of skill development. It is a statistic based on the age at which children learn to perform a skill independently for the first time. It is shown only as a means to measure if a child is progressing *significantly* behind the norm and therefore needs remedial or even medical help. Broad comparisons are meaningless because no two children grow at exactly the same pace or do well at all the same activities. A healthy, even talented child may excel in one area, be average in another and slightly below the norm in a third.

To promote progress *without* pushing, follow these important guidelines:

• Do not hold your kid back. If your child learns a skill sooner than the average, go directly to the next one in the sequence.

• Do not stop your child if she discovers a new skill on her own. Let's say that today your child discovers that she can not only grasp an object in her hand but release it, too—and suddenly that favorite rattle she picked up from the table is dropped on the floor. If your child spontaneously learns something new, don't stop her. But when you have a chance, look up the activity to be sure your child hasn't missed any steps in the progression of skill learning. If she has, go back and introduce the skipped activity while continuing to practice the other one as well.

• Sooner is not better. Thorough is best. There is no scientific evidence to indicate that early learning is advantageous. Furthermore, pushing your child to achieve a goal sooner than average, or just sooner than he's ready, may cause frustration and anxiety and may turn him off to physical activities for a long time to come.

Just adhere to the proper progression of skill learning and follow the instructions for recognizing learning readiness, and your child will get down the basics in his own time.

If your child is learning disabled

Children with learning disabilities commonly experience delays in motor skill development. For these chil-

dren the Gerard Method may be especially beneficial. If your child is learning disabled, just be sure to follow these special guidelines:
• Allow more time for practicing each skill. Each session should still be kept under 60 seconds, but increase the total number of lessons per week on a given skill, until your child can do it well.
• Do not be concerned about the average age learned for each skill since your child will probably progress more slowly. Just make sure to follow the correct progression of exercises. The sequence of skill development is the same for all children.

Also don't forget to introduce the colors to your child whenever he or she is ready. They are an especially good teaching tool for learning disabled children.

Making learning fun

Children make no distinction between learning and playing. The baby playing with his toes is learning where his body begins and ends; the toddler building with blocks is discovering about space and geometry; the preschooler tossing a ball is gaining firsthand experience of the laws of cause and effect. Children learn naturally, and with passion, but only as long as an activity remains fun and stimulating.

Skill learning should *never* be work for anyone concerned. The instant a "lesson" is no longer fun, stop immediately. Impatience, irritation, crankiness or lack of interest on the part of student *or* coach are cues to postpone the activity to a later time or date. Don't be misled by the carefully planned structure of the program: I promise that you can be serious about your child's development and still enjoy it.

The "Let's Play" section at the end of many activities suggests ways to introduce or practice new skills in the form of a game. These creative play techniques are just examples based on ones I invented for Christy as she was growing up. With a little imagination and enthusiasm, you can turn even a mundane chore into a game. I used to challenge Christy to play one-leg balance while I cooked and cleaned. "Look, *Mommy's* standing on one leg while she stirs," I would say. "Can *you* hold a spoon and stand on one leg?"

Remember, the purpose of the program is to give your kid a feel for movement—and a *positive* feeling about himself. This happens most readily when learning takes place in a safe, nonpressured, *playful* environment.

Okay, Coach, no more pep talks now. Just turn to the program and have *fun!*

4
HOW TO USE THE PROGRAM

The Gerard Method's step-by-step program of skill development consists of 96 activities, divided into three levels according to the age of the child and numbered in order of natural development. During the first year of life, the activities are designed to stimulate body awareness and increase muscle strength. Thereafter, they are divided into the following skill areas: balance, strength, coordination, fine motor skills and gross motor skills. On the average, one or two new activities are introduced each month during the first six years of a child's life.

Because the program requires only a modest commitment of time, it is easy to incorporate into your daily schedule. It is important to follow the program's structure to ensure thorough, well-rounded development, but it is not intended to be used as a rigorous drill routine. Even while keeping to the step-by-step instructions, you can use the activities as creative play techniques. Here's how:

• Set aside about 20 minutes once a week to review the activities and coaching guidelines on your own.
• Pick out two or three activities to introduce or practice in the coming week, and familiarize yourself with the instructions. Turn to the correct level for your child:

–Level One is birth to 12 months
–Level Two is 12 to 30 months
–Level Three is 28 to 72 months

Then check off the skills he has already mastered and identify the new activities he is ready to learn. Be sure he can do the required skills before you start on a new activity. As coach, you should not be standing with the book in your hand, reading off commands.
• Set aside a few brief time periods during the week when you will introduce a new activity or practice old ones. You need only 20-second "classes," a minute at most, to introduce new skills. Take your cues from your child. If your youngster cries out for more, that is your signal to spend more time on the skill.
• If you want to, keep a record of your child's progress in the "Steps to Skill Mastery" section. Use this data to complete the evaluation graphs in chapter 8 to monitor overall progress. Emphasize practice in those skill areas in which your child is weakest.

A guide to the activities

Once you have reviewed this chapter, the rest of the information you need to coach a skill successfully is contained in the step-by-step instructions for each activity.

All the activities follow the same format for easy understanding. Here is a basic guide to their structure:

Heading: The heading at the top of the page gives the age period during which the skill is learned. If your child is 8 months old, for example, then turn to the skills under the heading "6 to 9 Months." In Levels Two and Three, the heading also gives the skill category: Balance, Strength, Coordination, Gross Motor, or Fine Motor.

Title: Each activity has a name and a number. You will need to refer to the skill number if you use the evaluation graphs in chapter 8.

Goal: This is the description of what your child will learn to do. For the purposes of the program, your child has learned the skill the first time he accomplishes the goal without assistance.

Many activities have more than one goal. Usually, the additional goals are either an advanced stage or a variation of the initial skill. They are listed as separate objectives because they are important developmental milestones in themselves. When there is a significant difference in the age of skill learning between multiple goals, the later goal is noted again in its proper learning sequence. For example, if an activity for a 15-month-old has a second goal that is learned at 30 months, a reminder will appear in the "24 to 30 Months" section to return to the earlier activity.

---

65 REACH FOR THE STARS

GOAL: Your child balances on the balls of his feet for 2 seconds.

REQUIRED SKILL: Your child can balance on one leg for 2 seconds (52).

Your child has come a long way since the days when standing upright was still a precarious business, and he will enjoy the challenge to his secure sense of balance when he tries standing on tiptoe. This skill teaches him to become more aware of his center of gravity and develops ankle and leg strength, too.

Before you begin
• Clear a flat, matted surface.
• Be sure your child is barefoot.
• Have a toy available.
• Demonstrate the activity slowly.

Helpful hints
• Say "Rock" and "On tiptoe" to encourage your child to stand on his toes.
• Have your child focus forward on a toy placed 4 feet away.

Let's play
Cut out a paper star, or use a ball or other object, and hold it 8 to 10 inches above and slightly in front of your child's head. Ask him to stand on tiptoe and reach for the star.

STEPS TO SKILL MASTERY
1. Child balances on the balls of his feet for 2 seconds.
   Age learned _____ Average age learned: 32 months.
2. Child balances on the balls of his feet for 5 seconds.

1 Have your child stand with his feet shoulder width apart. Kneel behind him and support his back and rib cage. Encourage him to rock back and forth on his feet, then tell him to stop and balance on the balls of his feet and hold that balance for 2 seconds.

2 Repeat the activity, standing in front of your child and holding his hands in front of him at his chest level. Gradually release your grip until he balances independently on tiptoe for 2 seconds.

Before you continue, turn back to the goal listed below. This skill should be learned before you introduce the next exercise.
62/Dot to Dot, Goal 2

Required Skill: This entry gives the activity number and description of the skill or skills your child must know before he is ready for the current activity. This is really the first piece of information you should look at, because if your child cannot do the required skill for an activity, then he should not be doing it at all.

Introduction: The introductory paragraph usually includes a brief description of the skill and some background on its developmental importance. It may also include some pointers about coaching the skill.

Before You Begin: This section provides information about the play area and equipment needed to coach an activity effectively.

In Levels Two and Three, this section of an activity always ends with instructions for a demonstration of the skill. *This visual demonstration is the first step of skill learning and should never be skipped.* Present the activity using a doll if you cannot do it yourself.

Coaching Instructions and Illustrations: The coaching instructions always follow a three-stage process of skill learning. In the passive stage, the child does not actively initiate or control the movement, but is physically helped through it by the coach. In the second stage, the coach physically assists, or spots, the child's own attempts to do the skill. The final stage of learning is the active or independent level, in which the child learns to do the skill on his own, occasionally with light physical support from the coach.

To ensure proper learning:
• Always assist your child as instructed or illustrated.
• Never go on to the next step of the instructions until your child can do the previous step *well.* In some cases, especially in activities that have multiple goals, this may mean practicing one step of the skill for weeks or even months before your child will be ready to continue.
• Never skip a step or push your child to accomplish the activity sooner than he is ready.

Helpful Hints: These are general tips that usually include important safety and coaching reminders as well as information about where your child should focus while performing the skill; what verbal instructions to give your child; what stumbling blocks he may encounter; and how to give extra assistance when needed.

Steps to Skill Mastery: Your child will not learn a skill all at once but in steps over a course of time. The steps to skill mastery are the achievements on the road to proficiency. Use them as a checklist to make sure your child has not skipped a step in the learning process and to monitor his overall progress.

If you want, you can fill in the "age learned" where indicated. Your child has learned a skill the first time he achieves the goal on his own, *not* the first time he does it perfectly or consistently. If you want to keep a permanent record of your child's long-term development, you can chart it on the performance graphs in chapter 8.

Mastery is achieved when your child successfully performs a skill in eight out of ten tries over a period of time, and once this is accomplished, further practice is unnecessary.

Let's Play: These are examples of games I created to practice skills with my daughter. Feel free to invent some play techniques of your own. Even when playing, remember to provide coaching and assistance to your child as the instructions direct.

The coach's checklist

Now you have all the information you need to follow this program and start your child on his way to self-confidence and physical skill.

To make your job as straightforward as possible, I've put together a coach's checklist, a summary of the general coaching guidelines presented throughout this book. Read them over carefully before you start the activities, then refer to the checklist whenever you need to.

Prepare for the activity

☐ Check over the required skills to make sure your child is ready to learn the new skill.

☐ Review the new skill thoroughly before introducing it, so you don't have to hold the book as you coach.

☐ Clear a spacious, padded, well-lit area. Remove any sharp-edged furniture and protruding objects.

☐ Examine all equipment to be sure it is safe and in good working order.

☐ Create a quiet, relaxed atmosphere free of distractions. Keep all toys and equipment out of reach unless they are being used.

☐ Dress your child comfortably: for babies, as close to bare as possible, or in diapers to prevent accidents; for older children, loose-fitting clothes or leotards, and bare feet.

☐ Wait until your child is rested, refreshed and ready—and that goes for you, too.

☐ Present activities in an upbeat atmosphere, allowing for exploration, imitation and repetition. Let your kid know you enjoy them as much as he does.

Coach the activity step by step

☐ Do not push. Follow the 60-second rule for the maximum lesson time—until your child shouts for more. Children learn best through discovery: you be the guide while he is the explorer.

☐ Always follow the order of skills in the program, and never skip over an activity.

☐ Do not proceed to the next step until your child does the first one well.

☐ Demonstrate the skill with a doll if you can't do it yourself.

☐ Spot your child throughout every step as directed. Unless otherwise instructed, never stand in front of him or hold his hands above chest level when assisting.

☐ Keep your comments brief. Say "Ready" to start, "Very good" at the end and announce the name of the skill; for example, "Jenny, run!"

☐ Do not act alarmed if your child falls. Show him where his mistake was, and have him repeat the skill correctly.

Complete the activity

☐ Praise your child when he completes the skill. Always balance a positive comment with a constructive one following each attempt.

☐ Practice the skill until your child learns to do it *once* on his own. Then introduce a new activity, continuing to practice the old one until he can do it consistently well over a period of time.

☐ If you like, use the evaluation graphs to keep track of your child's progress. Provide extra help in areas where his skills are weak, to ensure that development is well rounded.

LEARNING WHAT THE BODY CAN DO

The first year of life is a period of unparalleled growth. At birth, a baby is totally helpless and physically dependent. His awareness is undifferentiated: when he is wet, the world is wet. The infant begins to realize he is separate from the world only as he experiences physical sensations that stimulate awareness of his body. Through sensory-motor experience, the newborn gradually learns what is "me" and "not me." Your child learns about his body and what it can do. His movements, at first reflexive and aimless, become conscious and purposeful. The baby achieves his first level of mastery—physical self-control.

Level One of the Gerard Method includes more than thirty exercises and activities designed to develop the baby's body awareness, sensory perception and strength, which are necessary to overall motor skill development.

At this first level, the baby masters movement on the blue axis, which runs vertically from head to toe. Rolling over, crawling and pulling to a stand all take place on the blue axis. These movements also enhance the ability to perceive the difference between the front and back of the body and to acquire a sense of up and down and left- and right-sidedness, which are needed for the later development of spatial awareness and spatial skills, including reading.

The Level One activities help babies to become aware of their bodies by stimulating their inborn motor reflexes, their senses and their muscle strength. In this way, babies learn what their bodies can do. The parent's role in holding, moving, massaging, rocking and otherwise touching and talking to the baby is critical at this level, and you will find that the activities offer an excellent opportunity to strengthen the bond between you and your child.

By his first birthday, that helpless newborn in your arms will be a more independent little person who is able to sit up and survey his surroundings, to pick objects up and, yes, drop them, to crawl over obstacles in pursuit of whatever thing has caught his eye and finally, on the brink of an exciting new exploration of his world, to stand on his own two feet. He will accomplish all these milestones with lots of prompting and assistance from you. The early months of his life may be the most demanding; he will require your constant attention and care. But out of that physical contact will grow one of the most fulfilling relationships of a lifetime.

Some special coaching tips for the new parent

The activities in Level One encompass the recognized developmental milestones in the first year of life. Always read the instructions carefully before you begin each activity, and refer to the checklist on page 19 for general coaching guidelines. In addition, here are some special points to keep in mind as you work with your baby throughout Level One.

• Keep lessons to a 20-second maximum. Especially in the early months, even 60-second lessons will be too much for your busy baby. Remember that everything in his world is new, and no one person, event or thing—outside of eating and sleeping—is bound to capture his attention for too long.

Note that most of the early activities suggest that you have your child focus on you. Infants have an inborn interest in the human face, and as long as your face is within his focal range, your newborn's attention will naturally go to you. In many early skills, his settled attention is the only response you can hope to get—and this is just as it should be. Within weeks, you may discover your child responding physically to you, even just to your presence or to the sound of your voice. By his third month, you can expect the thrill of receiving his first deliberate smile.

• Your baby will enjoy physical activities best if he is not wearing anything. Although you can leave a diaper on if you are worried about accidents, your direct touch is beneficial.

• Talk to your child as you do the activities, using short, simple phrases. Even though infants cannot understand the meaning of your words, your speech stimulates their language development and deepens the bonds between you.

• Stimulate your child's reflexes frequently. These preprogrammed "muscle memories" are important to your child's growing self-awareness as well as a vital steppingstone to development of movement control. Many of the activities in Level One are designed to stimulate your child's reflexes, and as long as your child is developmentally ready, feel free to practice them often.

1 TOUCH AND GROW

GOAL: Your child experiences awareness of her body parts.

REQUIRED SKILL: None.

At birth, babies do not sense that their bodies are separate from their environment. Gentle body massage is an excellent way to stimulate your newborn's self-awareness, as well as to strengthen bonding during the critical first 3 months of life. Research shows that touching and massaging may even enhance growth in low-birth-weight babies.

After your baby gets used to being massaged, she may respond by gurgling or by moving her arms and legs. Don't expect to see your infant smile until she is about 3 months old.

1 Lay your baby securely on her back. Using a piece of fabric or a smooth object, lightly massage your infant's feet, legs, belly, upper torso, hands, arms and head. As you stroke your baby with a gentle up-and-down motion, name each body part. Continue for 20 seconds.

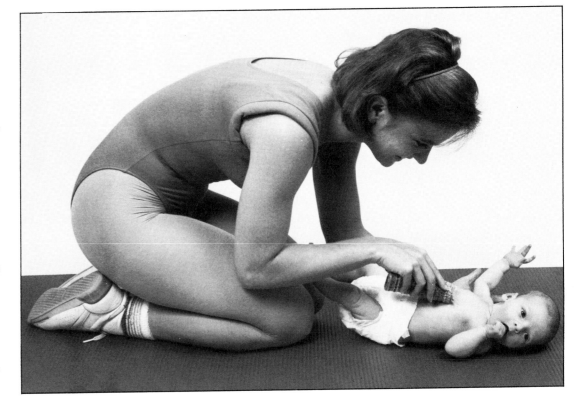

Before you begin
• Be sure your baby is undressed and the room is warm enough.
• Clear a flat, matted surface.
• Have available various textured materials, such as velvet, corduroy, denim, leather, silk, feathers, cotton balls, a smooth plastic toy and a soft sponge.

Helpful hints
• Before your baby responds directly to the activity, she will let you know she is paying attention by an alert expression or by being still.
• Use a gentle tone of voice to correspond to the feel of smooth or fine fabrics and a slightly stronger tone for coarser or firmer materials.

STEPS TO SKILL MASTERY
1. Child is attentive to the activity.
2. Child responds to the activity.
Age learned* _____   **Average age learned:** 0–3 months
* If you want to keep track of your child's progress, record this age on the appropriate graph in chapter 8.

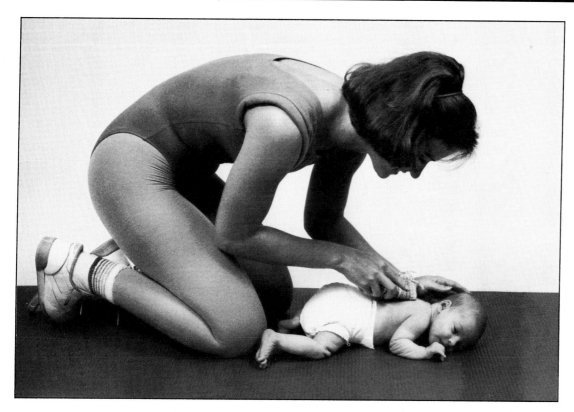

2 Turn your baby over on her belly and repeat step 1, stroking the heels, legs, buttocks, back, shoulders, elbows, arms, head, neck and ears.

Repeat steps 1 and 2, applying a firmer stroke, then using different materials.

2 HEADS UP

GOAL: Your child holds his head up when supported in a sitting position.

REQUIRED SKILL: None.

Unlike the previous exercise, which involved only passive movement, Heads Up gives your baby an opportunity to develop the back and neck strength necessary to hold his head up. You can safely introduce this activity by your baby's third week, but be sure to support his upper torso with your hands.

Before you begin
• Clear a flat, matted surface (optional).

1 On the mat or on your lap, place your child in a sitting position facing you. Firmly support his upper back and rib cage with your hands. Encourage your child to maintain eye contact with you.

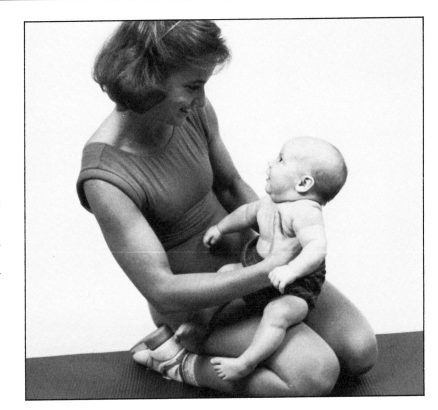

Helpful hint
• Before your child responds directly to the activity, he will let you know he is paying attention by an alert expression or by being still.

STEPS TO SKILL MASTERY

1. Child holds his head up momentarily.
2. Child holds his head up for several seconds.
   Age learned _____   **Average age learned:** 1 month
3. Child holds his head up consistently.

2 Blow softly on your child's face to encourage him to hold his head up. Say "Heads up." *Repeat three times in a row.*

3 LOOK AND SEE

GOAL: Your child focuses on an object held 6 inches in front of his eyes.

REQUIRED SKILL: None.

At birth, your baby's world appears blurred and confused because newborns cannot focus properly. As they learn to distinguish shapes, infants are more likely to move around and explore their environment. To stimulate shape recognition, you may introduce Look and See as early as 2 weeks after birth. It is natural that your baby's first attempts at focusing may result in crossing of the eyes.

Lay your child on his back on the mat. Hold a ½-inch object 6 inches directly in front of his eyes, saying his name to call his attention to it. Once he focuses on the object, move it forward and back, about 2 inches in each direction. Observe if he can maintain his focus even when the object moves only slightly.

Once your child can maintain his focus on a ½-inch object, repeat the activity using objects of increasing size.

Before you begin
• Clear a flat, matted surface.
• Have available a ½-inch, brightly colored object, such as a marble or some aluminum foil crumbled into a ball. *Never* leave this or other small objects within your child's reach when he is unattended.

Helpful hint
• Before your child responds directly to the activity, he will let you know he is paying attention by an alert expression or by being still.

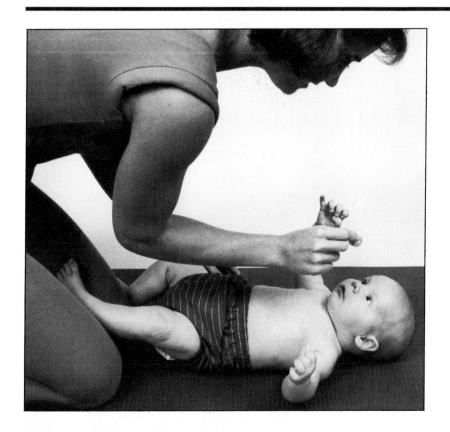

4 THE HEAD SHAKE

GOAL: Your child turns his head from side to side.

REQUIRED SKILL: None.

Newborns turn their heads from side to side in the same random way they move all parts of their body. Your child will be many months older before he willfully shakes his head to say no. That sort of deliberate movement requires more muscular strength and control. The Head Shake enables your infant to develop neck and back strength actively and at his own pace.

Before you begin
• Clear a flat, matted surface.
• Have available a brightly colored object or toy.

1 Place your child securely on his back. Hold a foil ball or a toy 10 inches directly in front of his eyes. Slowly move the object in an arc to the right until it touches the mat. Now move the toy all the way to the left until it touches the mat. Say "Look" to encourage your child to turn his head from side to side as he follows the moving toy.

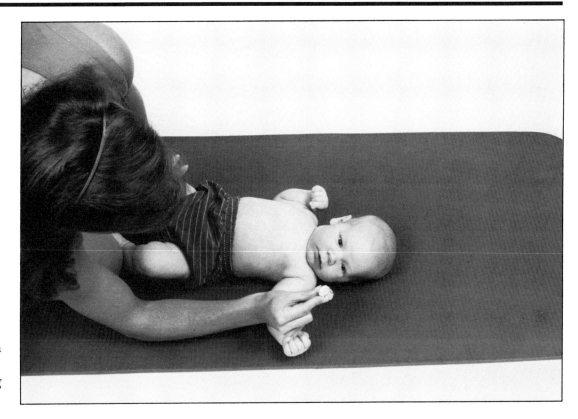

Helpful hints

• Before your child responds directly to the activity, he will let you know he is paying attention by an alert expression or by being still.

• It is *not* a goal of this exercise to maintain visual focus on the moving toy.

STEPS TO SKILL MASTERY

1. Child turns his head from side to side while on his back.
   Age learned _____   **Average age learned:** 1½ months
2. Child lifts up his head while on his belly.
3. Child turns his head from side to side while on his belly.

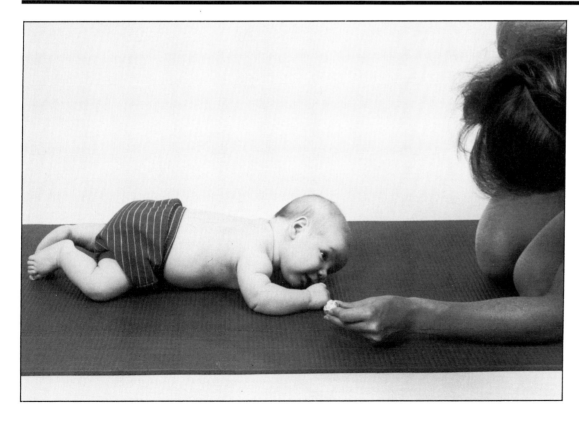

2 Turn your child over on his belly. Again, hold the object 10 inches directly in front of his eyes. Prompt him to lift up his head to see the toy. Once he can hold his head up, encourage him to turn his head from side to side as you move the object in an arc that ends about 10 inches from his ears.

5 ON YOUR FEET

GOAL: Your child pushes down on his feet and holds up his head when supported in an upright position.

REQUIRED SKILL: Your baby can hold up his head while being supported in a sitting position (**2**).

If you hold your baby upright, he will spontaneously press his feet against the ground, stiffen his legs and lock his knees. On Your Feet takes advantage of this push-down reflex to build muscle control and strength, particularly in his neck and back.

Before you begin
• Clear a flat, matted surface.

Helpful hints
• Before your child responds directly to the activity, he will let you know he is paying attention by an

Fully support your child's back and rib cage with your hands. Hold him in an upright position on the mat so he stiffens his legs and presses his feet down for a few seconds. Blow softly on his face to encourage him to hold up his head. Say "Heads up."

Repeat the activity on your lap or on a mattress, sofa or other soft surface.

alert expression or by being still.

• Your child's body will remain rounded and somewhat slack. He is not actually standing during this activity, and at no time should he be bearing any weight himself.

Let's play

Support your child in an upright position so he presses his feet against the ground. Lift him up about 6 inches and return him to a stand as you say "Up and down! Up and down!" Be sure you are fully supporting his weight at all times.

STEPS TO SKILL MASTERY

1. Child presses his feet against the mat when held upright.
2. Child holds up his head as he performs the push-down reflex.
   Age learned _____   **Average age learned:** 2 months
3. Child performs the activity on a mattress or on your lap.

6 FOLLOW THE TOY

GOAL 1: Your child tracks a horizontally moving object for a total of 6 inches.

GOAL 2: Your child tracks a horizontally moving object for a total of 12 inches.

REQUIRED SKILL: Your baby can hold up his head while being supported in a sitting position (**2**).

Visual problems, such as the inability to follow, or track, moving objects, have been associated with poor motor development. Moving objects appear fuzzy and unclear to a child who lacks the ability to control his eye muscles when tracking. Follow the Toy allows your child to exercise eye muscle control while providing you with a chance to monitor his tracking skills.

Before you begin

• Clear a flat, matted surface.
• Have available a brightly colored object or toy.

Place your child securely on his back on the mat. Hold the toy 6 inches in front of his eyes and call his name to encourage him to follow the object as you move it 3 inches to the right, back to the center, and then 3 inches to the left. Do this three times in a row.

Repeat the activity, holding the toy 10 inches from your infant's eyes.

Repeat the activity, holding the object 6 inches away and moving it horizontally for a total of 12 inches.

Helpful hints

• Before your child responds directly to the activity, he will let you know he is paying attention by an alert expression or by being still.

• If your baby's eyes cross as he attempts to follow the object, then it is too close to him. Increase the distance between his eyes and the object by 1 or 2 inches and then start the activity again.

• As your child's tracking skills improve, gradually hold the object farther away and increase the distance you move it horizontally.

STEPS TO SKILL MASTERY

1. Child attempts to follow the object, but cannot maintain focus.
2. Child maintains focus at a distance of 6 inches and follows the moving object a total of 6 inches to the right and left.
   Age learned _____   **Average age learned:** 2 months
3. Child maintains focus at a distance of 6 inches and follows the moving object a total of 12 inches to the right and left.
   Age learned _____   **Average age learned:** 3 months

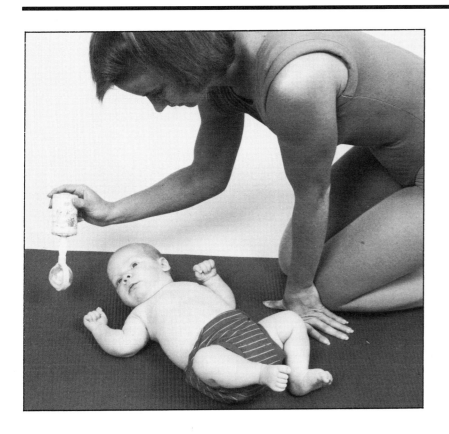

7 COCK THE HEAD

GOAL: Your child turns his head vaguely toward a sound.

REQUIRED SKILL: None.

In response to a new sound, infants typically become quiet and attentive at first, moving their eyes with interest. Then they may move their arms and legs excitedly and finally cock their heads vaguely in the direction of the sound. If your child does not respond to rattles or bells, tell your pediatrician, who may want to run some tests.

Before you begin
• Clear a flat, matted surface.
• Have available a rattle or small bell.

Helpful hint
• Before your child responds directly to the activity, he will let you know he is paying attention by an alert expression or by being still.

Place your child securely on his belly on the mat. Hold the rattle 6 to 10 inches from his right ear. Call his name as you gently and continuously shake the rattle for 10 seconds. See if your child turns his head slightly to the right in response to the sound.
Repeat the activity on the left side.
Repeat, using different sounds.
Place your child on his back and repeat the activity.

STEPS TO SKILL MASTERY
1. Child turns vaguely toward a sound on one side.
2. Child turns vaguely toward a sound on both sides.
   Age learned _____ **Average age learned:** 3 months
3. Child consistently turns toward various sounds.

8 THE COBRA

GOAL: Your child lifts up his head, chin and shoulders from a prone position.

REQUIRED SKILLS: Your child can turn his head from side to side (**4**) and can track a moving object (**6**).

A child's ability to balance in a sitting or standing position depends on successfully controlling and coordinating various muscle groups. The Cobra helps your baby develop the neck, upper body and back strength and the muscle control vital for later skills.

Before you begin
• Clear a flat, matted surface.
• Have available your child's favorite toy.

Helpful hints
• Before your child responds directly to the activity, he will let you know he is paying attention by an alert expression or by being still.
• Call your child's name to encourage him to focus on the toy.

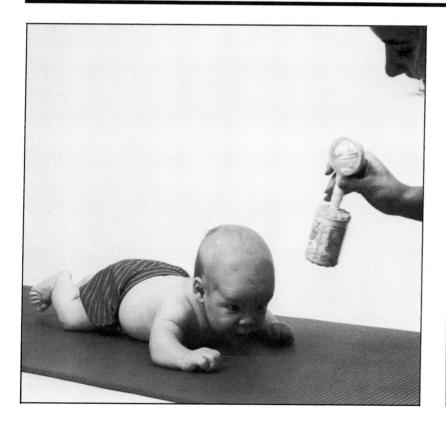

Place your infant on his belly. Kneeling in front of him, hold the toy about 6 to 10 inches in front of his eyes and slowly move it upward. Observe if he can lift his head, chin and shoulders off the mat to follow the object. Repeat three times in a row.

STEPS TO SKILL MASTERY
1. Child can lift up his head and chin only.
2. Child can lift up his head, chin and shoulders.
Age learned _____   **Average age learned:** 3 months

9 TILT AND TUMBLE

GOAL: Your child extends her arm to stop a fall when tilted sideways from a fully supported sitting position.

REQUIRED SKILL: Your child can hold up her head when supported in a sitting position (**2**).

Knowing how to stop her body from falling is vital to your child's safety. Tilt and Tumble provides an opportunity for your infant to exercise an important reflex and also to develop muscle control.

Before you begin
• Clear a flat, matted surface.

Helpful hints
• Encourage your child to focus forward.
• If you tilt your child too slowly, you will fail to produce a response.
• Never let your child actually fall.

Kneeling behind your child, place her in a sitting position and fully support her upper back and rib cage with your hands. Maintaining a secure grasp, quickly tilt her about 45 degrees to the right and say "Whoa!" as you stop. Your child should instinctively stick out her right arm to protect herself against a fall. If necessary, assist your child by extending her arm to the side.
Repeat for the left arm.
Repeat three times on each side.

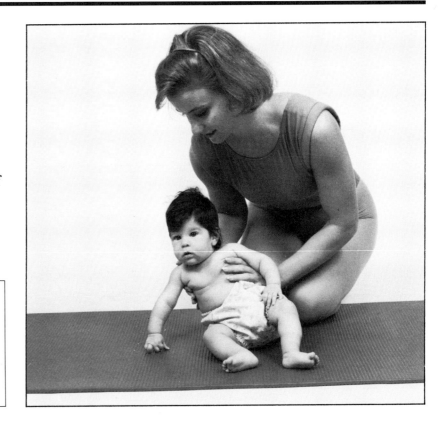

STEPS TO SKILL MASTERY
1. Child makes some attempt to extend her arm to the side.
2. Child extends her arm to the side to stop herself from falling.
   Age learned _____   **Average age learned:** 4 months
3. Child consistently extends her arm on either side.

10 THE DOWNWARD PARACHUTE

GOAL: Your child stretches her legs down, ready for a landing, when swiftly lowered to a standing position.

REQUIRED SKILL: Your child can push down on her feet when supported in a standing position (**5**).

The Downward Parachute provides an opportunity for your child to develop another important reflex.

Nature gives infants these reactions for safety and survival, and they should be exercised frequently.

Before you begin
• Clear a flat, matted surface.

STEPS TO SKILL MASTERY

1. Child moves her legs down slightly.
2. Child stretches her legs down stiffly to land.
   Age learned _____   **Average age learned:** 4 months
3. Child stretches her legs down to land three times in a row.

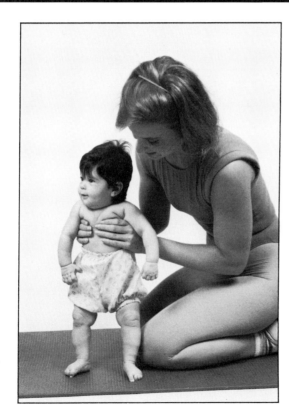

1 Place your child in a standing position so that her feet are pushing down against the mat. Encourage her to focus forward. Support her firmly with your hands, as shown.

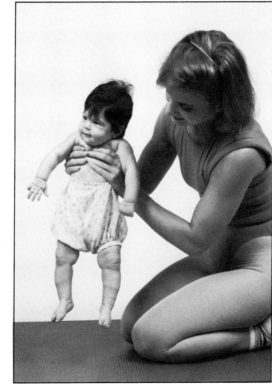

2 Swiftly lift your child about 12 inches, then say "Wheee!" as you quickly lower her again to a stand. See if she stretches her legs straight down to land. Repeat three times.

Repeat the activity with your child already lifted 12 inches above the mat in an upright position.

11 **ROLY-POLY**

GOAL: Your child rolls from her back to her side.

REQUIRED SKILLS: Your child can track a horizontally moving object (**6**) and can lift her head, chin and shoulders off the mat (**8**).

Any infant placed on her side will eventually roll over onto her stomach or her back simply because of the force of gravity, but not all babies will spontaneously roll from back to side. The ability to do this requires muscle control, coordination and effort. Playing Roly-Poly with your baby will help her to develop and practice this skill.

Before you begin
• Clear a flat, matted surface.
• Have available your baby's favorite toy.

Helpful hints
• If your child attempts to reach for the toy but does not roll over, place your hands under her hips and gently push forward to assist her.
• When you first attempt the exercise, if your child is unsuccessful in rolling onto her right side, try having her start by rolling onto her left side.
• If your child still has difficulty, place her diagonally across the middle of a slight incline so she will roll downhill.

Place your child on her back on the mat. Hold a toy 6 to 10 inches above your child's eyes and encourage her to look at it. Then move the toy slowly to her right so she must roll to her side to follow it. Repeat three times.
  Repeat the activity, moving the toy to your child's left.
  Repeat the activity on both sides.

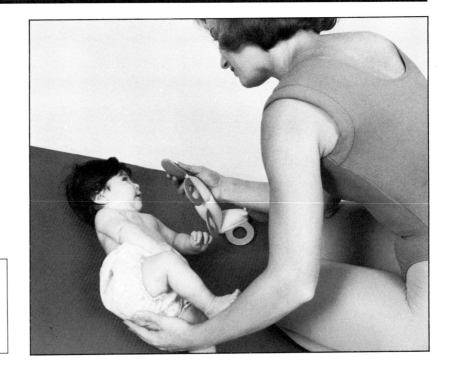

STEPS TO SKILL MASTERY
1. Child attempts to roll over to reach the toy.
2. Child rolls from her back to either side on a flat surface.
   Age learned _____   **Average age learned:** 4½ months

12 **SITTING PRETTY**

GOAL: Your child holds her back straight when supported in a sitting position.

REQUIRED SKILLS: Your child can hold up her head when supported in a sitting position (**2**) and can track a horizontally moving object (**6**).

Muscle control and strength, the prerequisites for balance, tend to develop from head to foot. A baby as young as 1 month old has enough neck strength to lift her head up when supported in a sitting position but not enough upper body and back strength to straighten her spine. Sitting Pretty promotes the development of back strength and muscle control necessary for sitting upright.

Before you begin
• Clear a flat, matted surface.
• Have available a brightly colored object or toy.

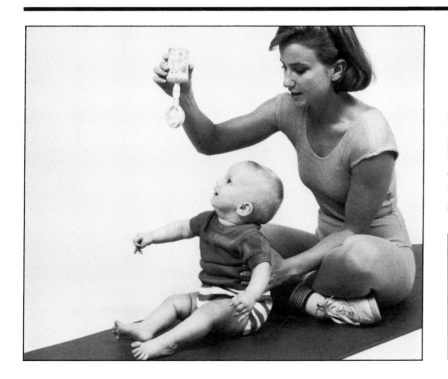

Place your child on the mat or on your lap in a sitting position, securely supporting her back and rib cage with one hand. With your free hand, hold a toy 6 to 10 inches in front of and slightly above her head. Call her name as you shake the toy to get her attention. Move it slightly higher to encourage your child to look up and straighten her back.

STEPS TO SKILL MASTERY
1. Child holds her head up when supported in a sitting position.
2. Child holds her back straight when supported in a sitting position.
   Age learned _____   **Average age learned:** 5 months

13 **LISTEN AND LOOK**

GOAL: Your child first turns and then inclines her head in the direction of a sound.

REQUIRED SKILL: Your child can turn her head vaguely toward a sound (**7**).

At 3 months old, a baby responds to a sound by cocking her head in its general direction. By 5 months, your child should be able to locate sounds more precisely—although still not directly—using her awareness, muscle control and coordination in a more integrated way. Listen and Look helps develop these important skills.

1 Hold your child securely with one hand in a sitting position on your lap or on the mat. With your free hand, hold a bell slightly above and to the right of her head.

Before you begin
• Clear a flat, matted surface (optional).
• Have available a bell, rattle and other household items, such as spoons, pot lids and keys.

Helpful hint
• Say "Listen" each time you ring the bell, shake the rattle or make another specific sound.

STEPS TO SKILL MASTERY

1. Child turns her head in the direction of the sound.
2. Child turns and then inclines her head in the direction of the sound.
   Age learned _____ **Average age learned:** 5 months
3. Child turns and inclines her head in the direction of various sounds.

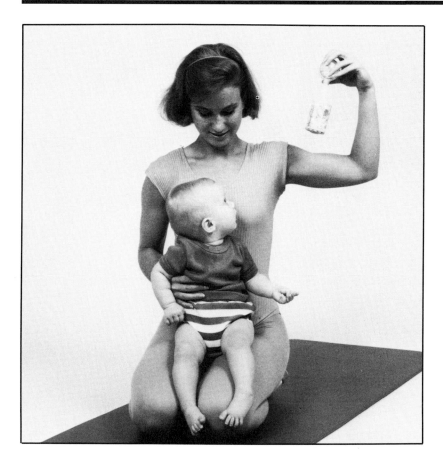

2 Ring the bell continuously for 10 seconds. Observe if your child *first* turns her head and *then* looks up toward the sound.

Repeat the activity on the left side.

Repeat, using different sounds and various locations. For example, produce one sound high and to the right and another low and to the left.

14 **THE ARCH**

GOAL: Your child raises her head and upper chest off the mat by pushing down on her hands and arms.

REQUIRED SKILLS: Your child can track a horizontally moving object (**6**) and can lift her head, chin and shoulders off the mat (**8**).

The Arch is an advanced form of an earlier skill in which your child lifted her head, chin and shoulders off the mat. Now your child will begin to use her arms to push her body off the ground. Achieving this arm strength and control is vital to your child's later ability to crawl.

Before you begin
• Clear a flat, matted surface.
• Have available a brightly colored toy.

Place your child on her belly on the mat and hold a toy 6 to 10 inches directly in front of her eyes. Slowly move the toy upward, encouraging her to follow it. See if she lifts her head and upper body by pressing down on her arms and hands. Repeat three times.

STEPS TO SKILL MASTERY
1. Child lifts her head and chin.
2. Child lifts her head and upper chest using her arms.
   Age learned _____   **Average age learned:** 5 months

15 **UP AND AWAY**

GOAL: Your child pulls up to a sitting position from lying down.

REQUIRED SKILL: Your child can sit with her back straight while slightly supported (**12**).

Up and Away provides new information to your child about up and down and improves muscular control required for balance. She will love the action-reaction effect of this game as you help her pull to a sit.

Before you begin
• Clear a flat, matted surface.

Helpful hints
• Say "Pull up" each time your child attempts or achieves the goal.
• Do not pull your child all the way up with your hands, but let her pull up by her own strength, using your hands for leverage.

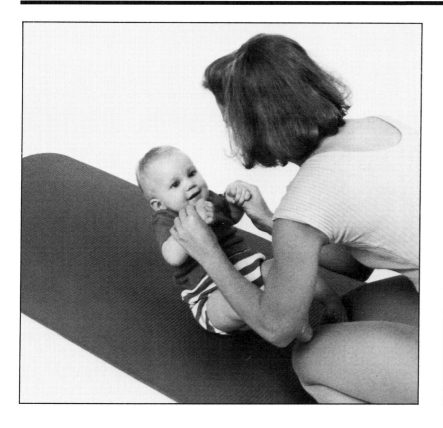

Place your child on her back on the mat. Kneel in front of her feet and encourage her to focus on you. Place your thumbs in her grasp and wrap your fingers securely around her hands. Gently assist her in pulling up to a sitting position, then lay her back down.

Repeat, gradually providing less assistance. Never release your grip entirely.

STEPS TO SKILL MASTERY
1. Child responds as you pull her to a sitting position.
2. Child pulls herself up to a sitting position.
   Age learned _____   **Average age learned:** 5½ months

16 WATCH IT GO

GOAL: Your child visually tracks a marble rolled for 3 to 6 feet.

REQUIRED SKILLS: Your child can track a horizontally moving object for 12 inches (**6**) and can lift up her head, chin and shoulders (**8**).

This activity teaches your child that a specific object will remain the same no matter where it is located. Playing Watch It Go, your child observes a marble change from a motionless to a moving state and back again without its being changed. This understanding is a milestone of development.

Before you begin
• Clear a flat, matted surface (optional).
• Have available a brightly colored ½-inch ball or

1 Place your child on her belly on the mat. Hold a ½-inch marble 6 to 10 inches in front of your child's eyes and encourage her to focus on it. Place it on the floor in front of her. Tell her to watch the marble as you gently roll it 6 feet forward and then stop it. Repeat three times.

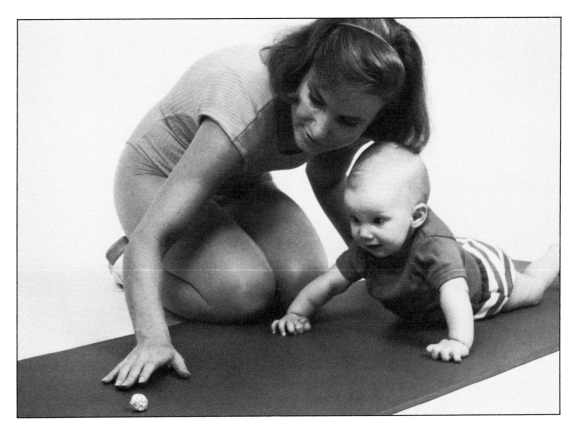

marble. *Never* leave this or other small objects within your child's reach when she is unattended.

STEPS TO SKILL MASTERY

1. Child tracks the marble for a few feet.
2. Child tracks the marble for at least 3 feet while on her belly.
   Age learned _____   **Average age learned:** 6 months
3. Child tracks the marble for 6 feet while held in a sitting position.

2 Place your child in a sitting position between your legs, with her back toward you. Repeat the activity, rolling the marble 6 feet forward.

17 **THIS AND THAT**

GOAL: Your child shifts her focus between two objects held 6 inches and 12 inches in front of her.

REQUIRED SKILLS: Your child can focus on an object held 6 inches in front of her (**3**) and can lift her head, chin and shoulders off the mat (**8**).

This and That presents a new focal challenge to your child that promotes better visual awareness as she learns to shift her focus from one object to another. It is also a game that promises to delight your baby.

Before you begin
• Clear a flat, matted surface.
• Have available two brightly colored toys.

1 Place your child on her back on the mat. Hold one toy 6 inches above her and the second toy 12 inches above. Shake the closer toy and encourage her to focus on it. Stop shaking the first toy and start shaking the second, and urge her to shift focus. Repeat three times.

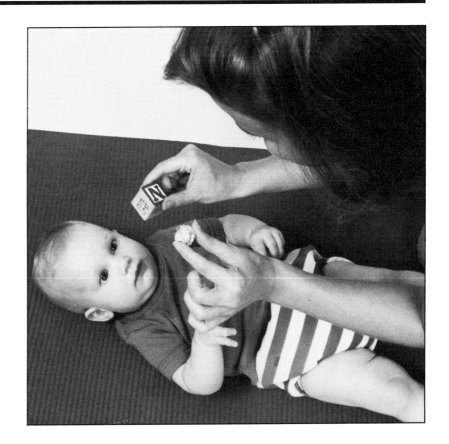

STEPS TO SKILL MASTERY

1. Child focuses on the first toy.
2. Child shifts her focus from one toy to the other while on her back.
   Age learned _____   **Average age learned:** 6 months
3. Child shifts her focus from one toy to the other while on her belly.

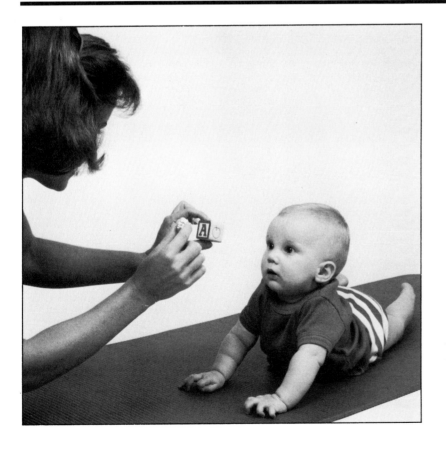

2 Place your child on her belly on the mat. Repeat the activity, holding the toys in front of her.

18 **ONE IN THE HAND**

GOAL: Your child deliberately grasps an object.

REQUIRED SKILLS: Your child can focus on an object held 6 inches in front of her (**3**); can lift her head, chin and shoulders off the mat (**8**); and will first turn and then incline her head toward a sound (**13**).

Once your child learns to reach out and grasp an object, she is able to bring the outside world to her and explore it in new ways. One in the Hand marks another stage of physical mastery, requiring both hand-eye coordination and fine motor skills.

Before you begin
• Clear a flat, matted surface.
• Have available a wooden block.

Place your child on her belly on the mat. Hold the block 6 inches in front of her to get her attention, then place it 3 inches from her reach on the mat. Say "Grab it" or "Get it" to encourage her to reach for the rattle.

Helpful hint
• Allow your child to reach for the block with which-
ever hand she favors. If necessary, place your hand
over hers and gently extend it toward the rattle to
assist her.

STEPS TO SKILL MASTERY
1. Child attempts to reach her arm forward.
2. Child deliberately grasps the rattle.
   Age learned _____   **Average age learned:** 6 months

19 **SWING AND SWAY**

GOAL: Your child holds some of her own weight and balances while supported in an upright position.

REQUIRED SKILL: Your child will push down on her feet and hold up her head when fully supported in an upright position (**5**).

Any infant of 2 or 3 months can balance on her feet for a few seconds if you stand her upright. But such balance is a simple demonstration of the laws of physics and has nothing at all to do with the infant's control. Swing and Sway develops body strength and true balance control by teaching your baby to control her body's movement.

Before you begin
• Be sure your child is barefoot.
• Clear a flat, matted surface.

Firmly support your child in an upright position on the mat with her back toward you, as shown. Say "Stand" as you loosen your grip slightly and let your child try to balance some of her own weight. *Don't release your grip entirely.* Assist her to an upright position as soon as she leans approximately 2 inches off center. Repeat three times.

Do the activity on different surfaces, such as your lap, a mattress, a couch cushion and the floor.

Helpful hints
• Encourage your child to focus forward.
• As your child gains the strength to balance some of her own weight, she will straighten her back and raise her arms.

Let's play
Support your child in a standing position. Maintaining a secure grip, tilt her body forward slightly on her feet and then move her body in a circle to the right. Say "Oooh!" as you circle her three times. Say "Stand" as you return her to her center of balance. Repeat the activity, this time circling her body to the left. Your child's feet should remain in place throughout the game.

STEPS TO SKILL MASTERY

1. Child supports some of her own weight while being held in a standing position on a flat, matted surface.
   Age learned _____   **Average age learned:** 6 months
2. Child supports some of her own weight while being held in a standing position on various surfaces.

20 THE ROCKING HORSE

GOAL: Your child balances on her hands and knees.

REQUIRED SKILL: Your child can lift her head and upper chest off the mat by pushing up on her arms and hands (**14**).

Children become safer crawlers if they first learn to control their balance while not moving. When your infant first gets up on all fours, she may fold her legs under her and sit on her feet. In doing The Rocking Horse, you will help her rock forward onto her hands. This motion will strengthen the quadriceps, the large muscles in front of the thighs that are needed to support the weight of her buttocks before she can crawl.

1 Place your child on her belly on the mat. Encourage her to focus on a toy placed 18 inches in front of her. Lift her onto her hands and knees by firmly supporting her back and rib cage, saying "Up" as you do.

Before you begin
- Clear a flat, matted surface.
- Have available your child's favorite toy.

Let's play
Place your child on her hands and knees as instructed in step 2. Sing "Rock-a-bye Baby" as you assist your child in a slight rocking motion. Continue for 20 seconds.

2 Gently move your child back and forth in a slight rocking motion three to five times. Gradually release your grip to let her try to maintain her balance independently.

21 **THE BELLY ROLL**

GOAL: Your child rolls from her back to her stomach.

REQUIRED SKILL: Your child can turn from her back to her side (11).

The Belly Roll builds upon the strength and motor skills your child developed when learning to roll from back to side. With the ability to roll over from back to stomach, your child gains greater mastery over her body, and can explore more of her world.

Before you begin
• Clear a flat, matted surface.
• Have available your child's favorite toy.

Place your child on her back on the mat. Hold her favorite toy 6 to 10 inches in front and to one side of her, and say "Get the toy" or "Roll over" as you encourage her to reach for it. As she does, slowly move the toy farther away from her so she must turn onto her stomach to get it. Do this three times.
Repeat the activity, moving the toy to your child's left.

Helpful hints

• Do not pull your child's arms. If she attempts to reach for the toy but does not roll over, place your hands under her hips and gently push forward to assist. If she needs further help, also push her shoulders.

• When you first attempt the exercise, if your child is unsuccessful in rolling in one direction, try having her roll onto the other side.

• If your child continues to have difficulty, try placing her on her back diagonally across the middle of an incline mat, with her head and one shoulder toward the uphill side. Sit at the bottom of the incline and do the exercise.

• Don't be concerned if your child wants to roll only onto one side. This is common and perfectly normal. Just keep trying.

STEPS TO SKILL MASTERY

1. Child attempts to reach the toy but does not roll over.
2. Child rolls over from back to stomach on a flat surface.
   Age learned _____   **Average age learned:** 6½ months

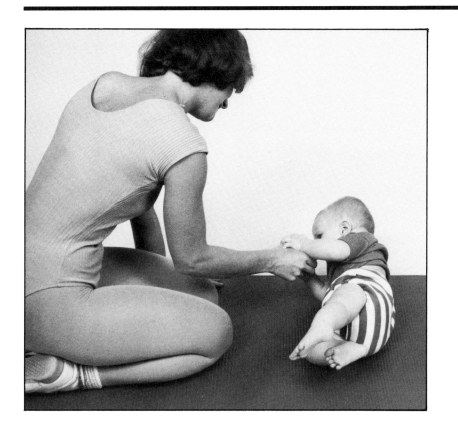

22 **SIT A BIT**

GOAL: Your child sits independently for 10 seconds.

REQUIRED SKILL: Your child can sit with his back straight when supported (**12**).

Children gain a different perspective once they learn to sit up. They also gain the free use of their hands to experiment and explore. Sit a Bit builds the muscle strength and upper-body control necessary for maintaining balance in a sitting position. With this achievement, your child can embark on a new phase of development—the mastery of fine motor skills.

Before you begin
• Clear a flat, matted surface.

Place your baby on the mat in a balanced sitting position. Kneel or sit behind him, firmly supporting his back and rib cage with your hands. Encourage him to focus forward. Say "Sit" as you loosen your grip to allow your child to try to balance independently. If he falls approximately 2 inches off center, resume your full support and return your child to his center of balance. Repeat three times.

Repeat the activity, placing your child in a sitting position on various surfaces, such as a mattress, your lap, and the low end of an inclined mat.

Helpful hint

• Be sure your child does the activity with help before he attempts it on his own.

Let's play

This game is similar to Swing and Sway (**19**), which develops balance when standing, except it is played while your child is sitting. Supporting your child in a sitting position, tilt his torso forward slightly and move it in a circular motion to the right. Say "Oooh!" as you circle him three times. Say "Sit" as you return him to the center. Repeat the activity, this time circling his torso to the left. Your child's buttocks should remain on the mat throughout the game.

STEPS TO SKILL MASTERY

1. Child balances in a sitting position momentarily.
2. Child sits independently on a flat surface for 10 seconds.
   Age learned _____ **Average age learned:** 7 months
3. Child sits independently on various surfaces.

23 FOUR ON THE FLOOR

GOAL: Your child moves into the crawling position from the sitting position.

REQUIRED SKILLS: Your child can balance on her hands and knees (**20**) and can sit independently (**22**).

Four on the Floor helps your baby develop the muscle control and coordination needed to move from one position to another. This is a breakthrough that will increase your child's self-confidence as she discovers a whole new world through her mobility.

Before you begin
• Clear a flat, matted surface.
• Have available your child's favorite toy.

 **1** Place your child on the mat in a sitting position. Offer her a toy and allow her to play with it for a few seconds.

Helpful hints

• Be sure your child does the activity with help before she attempts it on her own.

• Your child will fold one leg close to her body, extend the other leg slightly away and lift her body forward over the folded leg as she shifts from a sitting position to her hands and knees. While this may sound like a contortion to you, remember that a child's legs are proportionately much shorter than an adult's and therefore present much less of an obstacle.

• If necessary, hold your child's back and rib cage securely, and gently assist her into the crawling position.

STEPS TO SKILL MASTERY

1. Child attempts to move into the crawling position but stops herself.
2. Child moves into the crawling position.

   Age learned _____   **Average age learned:** 7½ months

2 Put the toy in front of her. Say "Come and get it" to encourage her to reach forward and crawl to the toy.

24 **STICKY FINGERS**

GOAL: Your child grasps an object using her thumb in opposition to her fingers.

REQUIRED SKILL: Your child can deliberately grasp an object (**18**).

Grasp this book with one hand. Notice how you naturally place your thumb around one side and your fingers around the other. This uniquely human ability to use the thumb in opposition to the fingers enables us to explore and manipulate the environment. Sticky Fingers gives your child a chance to test and exercise her grasp of various objects.

Before you begin
• Have available a toy block.

Helpful hint
• At first, your child may grasp the block with her thumb at a right angle to her fingers. If so, assist her by placing her thumb underneath the block, opposite her fingers.

Let's play
To play Sticky Fingers, offer your child many objects of different sizes, shapes and textures, one right after the other. See if your child can hold each one between opposing thumb and fingers.

Hold your child securely on your lap. Offer the block and say "Hold it" as you encourage her to focus on her hands and grasp it. See if she places her thumb and fingers on opposite sides of the cube. Repeat three times.

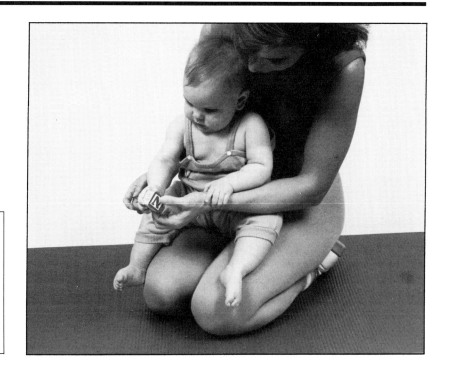

STEPS TO SKILL MASTERY

1. Child deliberately grasps the cube.
2. Child grasps the cube using her thumb in opposition to her fingers.
   Age learned _____   **Average age learned:** 8 months
3. Child grasps various objects using her thumb in opposition to her fingers.

25 **THE SOUND CHECK**

GOAL: Your child smoothly merges turning and inclining her head toward a sound.

REQUIRED SKILL: Your child will first turn and then incline her head in the direction of a sound (**13**).

At 5 months old, babies react to noises around them in a two-step process, by first turning and then inclining their head in the direction of a sound. Now, as sensory awareness and motor control become

more integrated, babies demonstrate a more immediate and coordinated physical response to the same stimuli.

Before you begin
• Clear a flat, matted surface (optional).
• Have available a bell, rattle and other household items, such as spoons, pot lids and keys.

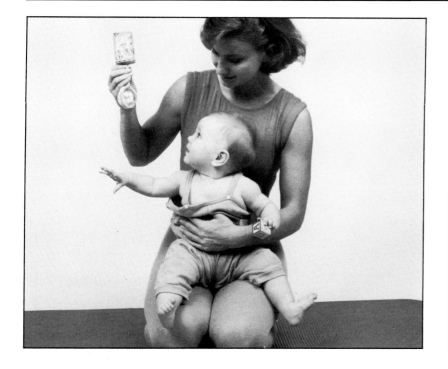

Hold your child securely with one hand in a sitting position on your lap or on the mat. With your free hand, hold a bell slightly above and to the right of her head, and say "Listen" as you ring it continuously for 10 seconds. Observe if your child *smoothly merges* turning and inclining her head toward the sound. Do the activity on the left side also.

Repeat, using different sounds and various locations. For example, produce one sound high and to the right and another low and to the left.

STEPS TO SKILL MASTERY
1. Child first clearly turns her head toward the sound and then looks up.
2. Child merges turning and inclining her head in the direction of the sound.
   Age learned _____ **Average age learned:** 8 months
3. Child merges turning and inclining her head toward various sounds.

26 THE PULL-UP STAND

GOAL 1: Your child pulls up to a stand from lying down.
GOAL 2: Your child pulls up to a stand from a sitting position.

REQUIRED SKILLS: Your child can pull to a sitting position from lying down (**15**) and can hold some of her own weight while supported in a standing position (**19**).

The Pull-up Stand is primarily a strength-building rather than a balancing activity. While first attempting it, you'll notice that your child pulls on your hands, pushes down on her legs and stiffens as she tries to bring her body to a stand in one motion. Only later will she develop the coordination and control to accomplish the goal in two steps, pulling first to a sit and then to a stand.

1 Place your child on her back on the flat mat. Kneel in front of her feet and encourage her to focus on you. Place your thumbs in her grasp and wrap your fingers securely around her hands. Say "Up" or "Stand" as you pull your hands slightly toward you to assist her to a standing position.
   Repeat the activity on the inclined mat, with your child's feet pointing downhill.

Before you begin
• Clear a flat, matted surface and a matted, slightly inclined surface.
• Be sure your child is barefoot.

Helpful hints
• A span of time is usually needed in order to learn each step of the skill.
• Do not pull your child all the way up with your hands. Let her pull up with her own strength, using your hands for leverage.

STEPS TO SKILL MASTERY
1. Child pulls herself from a lying down position to a standing position on a flat surface.
   Age learned _____   **Average age learned:** 8 months
2. Child pulls herself from a lying down position to a stand on an incline.
3. Child pulls herself from a sitting position to a stand on a flat surface.
   Age learned _____   **Average age learned:** 9½ months
4. Child pulls herself from a sitting position to a stand on an incline.

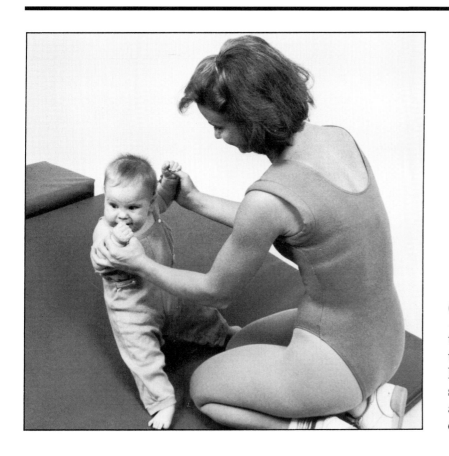

2 Place your child in a sitting position on the flat mat and help her up to a stand. Also do this activity on the inclined mat.

27 THE FORWARD PARACHUTE

GOAL: Your child extends his arms to brace himself as his body moves forward and down toward the floor.

REQUIRED SKILL: Your child can support some of his own weight when held in a standing position (**19**).

Reaching out to brace the body against a fall is an inborn reflex. The Forward Parachute is designed to stimulate this reflex before your baby learns to balance and walk. It provides the sensations of falling and bracing in an environment that is both fun and safe, so that when he actually takes a spill, the experience won't be unfamiliar or scary.

Before you begin
• Clear a flat, matted surface.
• Have available a soft toy.

1 Kneel down and place your child in a standing position, supporting his back and rib cage with your hands. Encourage him to focus his attention on a toy placed on the mat. Slowly lower your child forward toward the mat, saying "Stop" or "Reach" as you do. See if he extends his arms to brace himself. Repeat three times.

Let's play

Most children love the sensation of flying through the air Superman-style, as long as they are safely secured in an adult's arms. In this game, your child has the fun of flying and learns how to come in for a safe landing, too. To play, kneel and hold your infant in your forearms, with his stomach facing downward. While holding him securely, bring him forward and down to the floor in your arms. Say "Wheeeee!" as you fly him through the air, and exclaim "Stop!" or "Land!" as he reaches out his arms toward the floor. Be careful!

STEPS TO SKILL MASTERY

1. Child makes some attempt to reach forward and brace his arms when lowered to the floor from a standing position.
2. Child reaches forward and braces his arms when lowered from a standing position.
   Age learned _____   **Average age learned:** 8½ months
3. Child reaches forward and braces his arms when lowered from a height of 2 feet.
4. Child reaches forward and braces his arms when lowered from various heights.

2 Now put one arm under your child's chest and the other arm under his thighs. Lift him about 2 feet off the mat. Slowly bring your child forward and down toward the mat as you say "Stop" or "Reach."

Repeat the activity three times, gradually increasing the height and speed of the motion toward the floor.

28 EYES ON THE BALL

GOAL: Your child visually tracks a marble rolled for 12 feet.

REQUIRED SKILL: Your child can track a marble rolled for 3 to 6 feet (**16**).

The ability to clearly locate and recognize objects at a distance is critical to your child's safety once she starts to crawl and explore her surroundings. Eyes on the Ball is a tracking activity that builds on earlier skills to promote specific focusing and depth perception.

Before you begin
• Clear an area on the floor.
• Have available a brightly colored ½-inch ball or marble. *Never* leave this or other small objects within your child's reach when she is unattended.

1 Place your child on her belly on the floor. Hold a ½-inch marble 6 to 10 inches in front of her eyes and encourage her to focus on it. Place the marble on the floor in front of her. Say "Look" or "Watch it" as you gently roll the marble 12 feet forward and then stop it. Repeat three times.

• Have a coaching partner to assist you with the activity.

Let's play

This game provides practice in tracking objects within a specific visual field. Gather together several balls or other round objects of varying sizes and colors. Place your child on her belly on a clean floor and put all the balls in front of her. Roll them one at a time for 10 to 12 feet and encourage her to follow them visually. Repeat the game with your child supported on the floor in a sitting position.

<table>
<tr><td colspan="2">**STEPS TO SKILL MASTERY**</td></tr>
<tr><td>**1.**</td><td>Child tracks the marble for a few feet.</td></tr>
<tr><td>**2.**</td><td>Child tracks the marble for at least 10 feet while on her belly.</td></tr>
<tr><td></td><td>**Age learned** _____ **Average age learned:** 9 months</td></tr>
<tr><td>**3.**</td><td>Child tracks the marble for 12 feet while held in a sitting position.</td></tr>
</table>

2 Sit on the floor in a straddle position and place your child in a sitting position between your legs with her back toward you. Repeat the activity, letting your coaching partner stop the rolling marble.

29 THE CRAWLER

GOAL: Your child crawls forward 4 feet on a flat surface.

REQUIRED SKILLS: Your child can balance on his hands and knees (**20**) and can move into a crawling position from a sitting position (**23**).

With crawling comes mobility at last. For your child, that means new-found freedom and mastery. Once he learns to crawl, your child has greater access to things he wants and a means by which to take control of his own needs. For you, it means it's time to keep a closer eye on your little one! During this critical period, it's important not to confine your baby to a playpen or walker all day, or to otherwise overly restrict his mobility.

1 Place your child belly down near the top of the inclined mat with his feet pointing uphill and kneel beside him. With one hand, bounce the toy on the bottom of the incline and say "Come on" or "Crawl" to encourage him to go to it. To assist him, place the palm of your free hand flat against the soles of his feet. Continue the activity for 3 minutes.

Before you begin

• For steps 1 and 3, set up a matted, slightly inclined surface; for step 2, clear a flat, matted surface.
• Have available your child's favorite toy.

Helpful hint

• Do not try to push your child forward. Provide leverage only as your child pushes his feet against your hand in order to crawl.

2 Place your child belly down on a flat mat and do the activity.

3 Place your child belly down near the bottom of the inclined mat with his feet pointing downhill. Repeat the activity, having your child crawl *up* the incline.

30 **THE HANDY STAND**

GOAL 1: Your child stands while holding on to furniture.

GOAL 2: Your child climbs to a standing position from a sitting position while holding on to furniture.

REQUIRED SKILLS: Your child can lift his head and upper body off the mat by pushing down on his hands (**14**); can hold some of his own body weight when supported in a standing position (**19**); can sit independently for 10 seconds (**22**); and can move into a crawling position from a sitting position (**23**).

The Handy Stand is primarily a strength-building rather than a balancing activity. It enables your child to develop the muscle control to fully support his own weight, using his legs to push against the floor and his arms to hold his upper body. Although he must still hang on to the furniture to keep his balance, your child will discover for himself that he can stand without help from Mom or Dad—a big step toward self-sufficiency.

Before you begin

• Clear the area around two pieces of furniture that are waist high to your child. One should be hard,

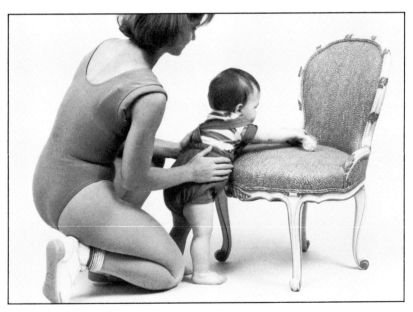

1 Support your child in a standing position directly in front of the upholstery so he is almost leaning against it. Place the toy on the upholstery and then place his hands by the toy. Be sure his attention is on the toy.

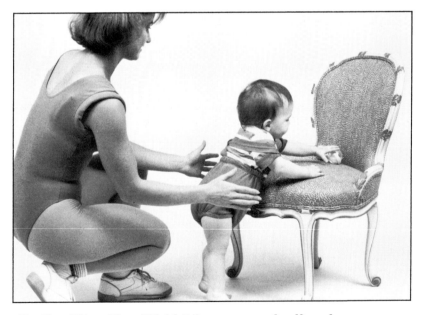

2 Say "Stand" or "Hold it" as you gradually release your grip, encouraging your child to hold on to the upholstery for support as he tries to get the toy. Repeat three times.
Do the activity again, using a hard piece of furniture.

such as a coffee table, chair or stool, and the other upholstered, such as a low couch, bed, ottoman, securely stacked mattresses or cushions. Avoid furniture with sharp edges.
• Have available your child's favorite toy.

Helpful hints

• A span of time is usually needed in order to learn each step of the skill.
• Be sure your child does the activity with help before he attempts it on his own.
• Always keep your hands near your child's back and rib cage to assist him if needed.

• Some children first move into the crawling position before they attempt to climb to a standing position.

STEPS TO SKILL MASTERY

1. Child stands by himself while holding on to the upholstery.
   Age learned _____   **Average age learned:** 9 months
2. Child stands by himself while holding on to various pieces of furniture.
3. Child climbs to a stand while holding on to upholstery.
   Age learned _____   **Average age learned:** 11 months
4. Child climbs to a stand while holding on to various pieces of furniture.

3 Place your child in a sitting position 1 foot away from the upholstery (or cushions). Show him the toy and place it on the upholstery.

4 Encourage him to climb to a standing position to reach the toy. Keep your hands near his back and rib cage in case he loses his balance. Repeat three times.
Do the activity again, using a hard piece of furniture.

31 PAT-A-CAKE

GOAL: Your child deliberately claps his hands.

REQUIRED SKILL: Your child can deliberately grasp an object (**18**).

Motor development plays a vital role far beyond the physical in shaping your child's sense of self. The development of fine motor ability is particularly important because the hands are a significant tool for self-expression. Pat-a-Cake fosters a coordination skill your child will use again and again as a means to express delight.

Before you begin
• Clear a flat, matted surface (optional).
• Demonstrate the skill slowly. Say "I clap" so your child will watch your hands.

Let's play
Place your child securely in a sitting position on your lap. Sing a pat-a-cake song as you clap his hands together.

Place your child securely in a sitting position on the mat or on your lap. Hold his hands, clap them together and say "Clap" to encourage him to be aware of his hands. Gradually release his hands to allow him to clap by himself.

STEPS TO SKILL MASTERY

1. Child makes some attempt to clap.
2. Child claps by himself.
   Age learned _____ **Average age learned:** 9½ months
3. Child claps several times when asked.

32 THE GOOD LISTENER

GOAL: Your child turns his head in a direct diagonal movement toward a sound.

REQUIRED SKILL: Your child can smoothly merge turning and inclining his head toward a sound (**25**).

The Good Listener monitors the continuing growth of hearing and listening skills, which are essential for safety as well as for all learning and language development. In earlier activities, your child reacted to sounds in a two-step process, first turning and then inclining his head in the direction of the noise. As he masters this activity, he will be able to accomplish the same response with one direct turn of the head.

Before you begin
• Clear a flat, matted surface.
• Have available a bell, rattle, and other household items, such as spoons, pot lids and keys.

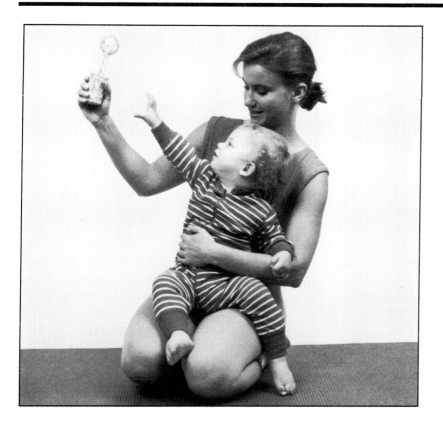

Place your child in a sitting position on the mat and kneel behind him, or put him on your lap with his back to you. Encourage him to focus forward. Then say "Listen" as you hold a bell 6 inches above and to the right of his head and ring it continuously for 20 seconds. Observe to see if your child immediately turns and looks at the sound in one direct, diagonal movement.

Repeat the activity on the left side.

Repeat step 1, using different sounds and various locations. For example, produce one sound high and to the right and another low and to the left.

STEPS TO SKILL MASTERY
1. Child turns and inclines his head toward the sound.
2. Child turns his head in a direct, diagonal movement toward the sound.
   Age learned _____   **Average age learned:** 10 months
3. Child turns his head in a direct, diagonal movement toward many types of sounds.

33 **CRAWL AND CLIMB**

GOAL: Your child crawls up and over an obstacle.

REQUIRED SKILLS: Your child can move from a sitting position to a crawling position (**23**) and can crawl well (**29**).

Crawl and Climb creates an added challenge for your new crawler, presenting him with an obstacle course of pillows and cushions. Now, to get from here to there, your child must discover how to climb up, across and down an uneven, shifting surface. The effort will sharpen his problem-solving abilities and improve his strength, balance and coordination.

Place two soft pillows several feet apart in a path on the floor. Place your child in a sitting position a few feet from the first pillow. Move a toy back and forth from the floor to the pillow to get his attention, and say "Crawl up" or "Crawl over" to encourage him to come to the toy. Continue bouncing the toy slightly ahead of your child's reach to motivate him to crawl up and over the first and then the second pillow.

Repeat the activity, using firm cushions in place of the pillows.

Before you begin

• Clear an area on the floor.

• Have available your child's favorite toy and some standard pillows and firmer cushions (no more than 2½ inches thick).

Helpful hint

• If necessary, press your free hand against the soles of your child's feet to assist him in crawling.

STEPS TO SKILL MASTERY

1. Child crawls up and over a standard pillow with assistance.
2. Child crawls up and over a standard pillow without help.
   Age learned _____   **Average age learned:** 11 months
3. Child crawls up and over a firm cushion without help.

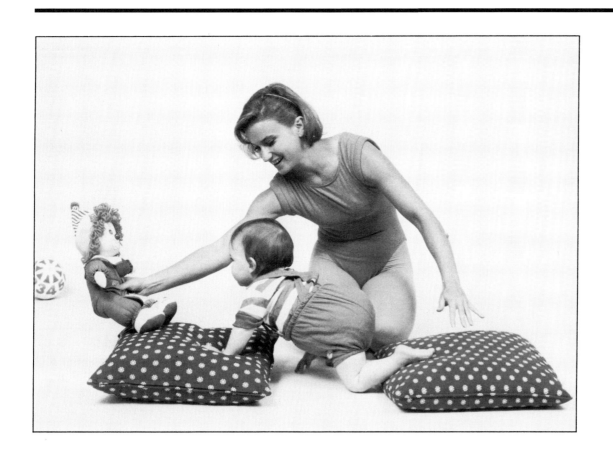

34 THE PUPPET WALK

GOAL: Your child walks with assistance.

REQUIRED SKILL: Your child can support his own weight when held in a standing position (**19**).

Walking is the basis of all further gross motor development, so it's vital that a child learn to do it properly. Your child will soon discover that the trick to this liberating new skill is to move forward and keep his balance at the same time. He'll have a much easier time learning to do this if he's barefoot. Shoes challenge a child's walking skill as much as high heels challenge an adult's.

Before you begin
• Clear a flat area on the floor.
• Demonstrate the skill slowly. Say "I walk" to prompt your child to watch you.

Stand or kneel behind your child. Support him by placing your thumbs and palms on his back and your fingers around his sides and rib cage (as if you were about to knead his back). Encourage your child to focus ahead. Say "Walk" as you urge him to step forward. *Do not push.*

Repeat the activity, holding your child's hands out to the side at chest level.

Helpful hints

• Do not stand in front of your child. If he relies on seeing you to learn the skill, he will be poorly prepared to walk on his own.

• Never hold your child's hands above chest level when assisting him, because it disturbs his natural center of balance.

Let's play

• The Puppet Walk gives a child some sense of walking before he has had the experience of doing it on his own. To play, support your child's back and rib cage with your hands and place him in a standing position with his back to you and his feet on top of yours. Say "Walk" as you step forward slowly.

STEPS TO SKILL MASTERY

1. Child takes one step forward while his back and rib cage are supported.
2. Child takes several steps forward while his back and rib cage are supported.
   Age learned _____   **Average age learned:** 11 months
3. Child walks forward well while his hands are held.

35 **SWIVEL SEAT**

GOAL: Your child maintains his balance in a sitting position when he turns to pick up a toy.

REQUIRED SKILLS: Your child can deliberately grasp an object (**18**) and can sit independently (**22**).

For adults, sitting is second nature. It is something we do effortlessly, usually in order to do something else—eating, writing, or simply relaxing. Indeed, sitting barely rates as an activity at all. For the child who has just learned to do it on his own, however, this simple act is an Olympic event, requiring total concentration and effort just to maintain balance. Swivel Seat tests your child's ability to sit upright even while moving other parts of his body.

Before you begin
• Clear a flat, matted surface.
• Have available a favorite toy.

Place your child in a sitting position on the mat with the toy to his right. Say "Get the toy" to encourage him to reach for it with either hand. If he loses balance, place your hands around his back and rib cage.

Repeat with the toy to your child's left side.

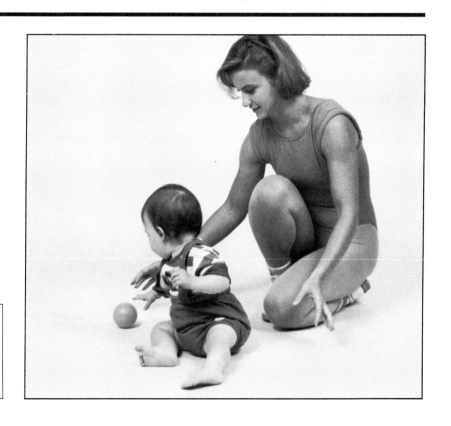

STEPS TO SKILL MASTERY
1. Child turns and reaches for the toy with assistance.
2. Child turns and reaches for the toy by himself.
   Age learned _____   **Average age learned:** 11 months

36 **PULL A PEG**

GOAL: Your child pulls a peg from a peg board with a "mature" grip.

REQUIRED SKILL: Your child can grasp an object using his thumb in opposition to his fingers (**24**).

Hand strength is an essential component of overall body strength, yet it is often the most neglected. Pull a Peg develops a "mature" grip, which uses precise thumb-finger opposition and is more powerful and purposeful than a child's first grasp. This kind of hand strength and dexterity is the foundation for later, more precise skills like writing.

Before you begin
• Have available a peg in a peg board.
• Demonstrate the skill slowly. Place the peg board in front of your child and say "I pull" as you remove the peg using your thumb and forefingers.

Helpful hints
• Encourage your child to focus on his fingers as he pulls the peg.
• If necessary, place your fingers over his to assist him.

Seat your child on your lap. Push the peg snugly into the peg board. Hold the board for your child and say "Pull" as you urge him to grab the peg and pull it out. See if he is pulling tightly with his thumb and fingers. Repeat three times.

STEPS TO SKILL MASTERY
1. Child pulls out the peg using a strong, "mature" grip.
   Age learned _____ **Average age learned:** 12 months
2. Child pulls out the peg three times in a row.

37 **CLAP THE BALLOON**

GOAL: Your child tries to catch a balloon dropped from just above his reach.

REQUIRED SKILLS: Your child can visually track a moving object (**28**) and can clap his hands (**31**).

Clap the Balloon helps develop your child's ability to connect what he sees with what he does, which is called hand-eye coordination. Remember, the goal here is not to catch the balloon but *react* to it and *make an attempt* to catch it. At this age, your child's motor system may not yet be mature enough to grasp the balloon successfully.

Before you begin
• Have available a balloon 5 to 8 inches in diameter.
• Demonstrate the skill slowly, saying "I catch" as you do.

1 Hold your child securely in your lap in a sitting position with his back against you. Show him the balloon. Hold it 2 inches above his reach and encourage him to look at it.

Helpful hints

• Children seem to respond to the idea of clapping the balloon as a means of catching it, since clapping is a skill they already know.

• It will be easier to assist your child in clapping if you have a partner hold the balloon.

STEPS TO SKILL MASTERY

1. Child watches the balloon fall to the ground.
2. Child attempts to catch the balloon.
   Age learned _____   **Average age learned:** 12 months
3. Child catches the balloon.

2 Place one hand on your child's forearm. Say "Catch the balloon" or "Clap the balloon" as you release it with one hand and help him clap it with the other. Repeat three times.

Repeat the activity, dropping the balloon from 4 inches above your child's reach.

38 THE PERFECT BALANCE

GOAL: Your child balances in a standing position for 10 seconds.

REQUIRED SKILL: Your child can pull himself up and stand while holding on to furniture (**30**).

The staggering rate of growth in your child's first year of life will never again be duplicated. In just 12 months, he has learned to recognize sounds and objects, perceive space and movement, hold things, drop things, and express himself with his hands. He has also learned to roll over, sit up, crawl, and climb to a stand. Now your child will apply his newly acquired strength, balance and coordination to achieve the final goal of the first year's development: upright balance.

Before you begin
• Be sure your child is barefoot.
• Clear a flat, matted surface.

1 Kneeling behind your child, hold him in a standing position with his feet shoulder width apart. Say "Stand" or "Balance" as you release your grip slightly, allowing him to support most of his own weight.

Helpful hints
• Assist your child back to the upright position as soon as he falls 10 degrees (approximately 2 inches off center) in any direction.
• Gradually release your grip, allowing your child to balance independently. Keep your hands near his back and rib cage in case you need to catch him.

Let's play
This game is just like Swing and Sway (**19**), with two exceptions. Now your child is mature enough to participate more purposefully, and strong enough to control his own movement and balance more suc-cessfully. To play, support your child in a standing position. Tilt him forward about 10 degrees. Then move him around in a circle two or three times as you make wind sounds like "Whoosh!" or "Wheeee!" Say "Stop" or "Balance" as you quickly return your child to an upright position. Children adore this game. After a few trials they will gleefully antici-pate when the wind will stop. As your child's skill develops, he may initiate the game independently, imitating the sound of the wind and exclaiming "Stop!" as he experiments with his own balance control. Always maintain your spotting position, even when playing the game.

2 Lean your child slightly to the right, back, left and forward. Then return him to the upright position. Repeat three times.

STEPS TO SKILL MASTERY
1. Child balances for a few seconds.
2. Child balances for 10 seconds.
   Age learned _____   **Average age learned:** 12½ months
3. Child balances while holding a toy.

LEARNING TO WALK, RUN AND JUMP

Level Two of the Gerard Method spans the period from 1 to 2½ years of age. It consists of 21 activities to help toddlers master walking, running, jumping, kicking and throwing—that is, those skills that naturally develop as a result of our species's unique upright posture.

Precisely because they can stand upright, toddlers begin to learn all the ways they can get into mischief. Their increased manual dexterity enables them to take things apart. Their newfound mobility enhances their sense of themselves as separate from the world. Able to move around and explore, they look at things close up, touch them, taste them and smell them to learn more about them. They can act on their environment in new ways, achieving a greater sense of independence and confidence.

In terms of the Body Color Theory, the toddler masters the ability to translate, or move along, the three body axes in this stage of the program. Walking and running are yellow axis translations; stepping to the side is a red translation; and jumping is a blue translation.

At Level Two, your child also develops hand-eye (catching and throwing) and foot-eye (kicking) coordination skills as well as fine muscle control of the hands. The ultimate accomplishment of this stage is a jump on the blue axis—your child's first "flight-phase" skill. With this ability, he achieves a new level of freedom in movement.

Some special coaching tips

This stage of life is the "crazy" time. Your child has just begun to develop control of his movements but at the same time is not yet completely independent. He can walk around on his own, but not *too* far on his own. He can manage to climb a few steps and even climb to places you'd much prefer he didn't go. He can manage to disassemble just about anything you'll let him hold—maybe even take off some clothes on a whim—but he can't put things back together or get dressed when he's told. By the time he is 2 or 2½, he will be running and jumping a bit, but not so well that he doesn't get an occasional bump or bruise. After all, he's not called a toddler for nothing.

This is an age when you really must pay close attention to your child, because many times his ability to move around his world will greatly exceed his understanding of it. As always, carefully follow the instructions for the individual activities as you go through Level Two, and refer to the checklist on page 19 for general coaching guidelines. Also keep these additional tips in mind:

• Always demonstrate skills slowly and with exaggerated effort. Visual demonstrations are very valuable starting at this age, because toddlers learn physical skills through imitation. Keep in mind, too, that the *process* of movement is far more important in Level Two than the actual performance of it. When teaching your child how to throw, kick, or stand on one leg, you need only be concerned that he learns the basic motion or achieves the basic balance. If the ball doesn't reach the target, if his arms aren't straight or his toes aren't pointed at this stage of learning, it doesn't matter; he will learn how to refine his skills in Level Three.

• Encourage your child to focus. Your youngster is first learning how to coordinate what he sees with what he does. He is barely conscious of the fact that he needs to look where he is going. A focal point helps your child to understand exactly where you want him to move his body and where he should look while he's doing it.

• Introduce "Let's Play" activities with direct instructions and, for fun, use exaggerated gestures and speech. In terms of skill learning, toddlers are quite literal-minded, and imaginary games have little or no appeal. Also remember to be patient, because your youngster will not always be able to understand your directions and immediately translate them into the correct movements. Although his vocabulary is starting to grow, the exact meaning of new words may still elude him.

Be patient, too, because this is the "terrible" age when everything must happen *now,* and your child is apt to get frustrated or lose interest quickly unless he is quite ready in his own mind to do what you are asking.

39 THE FIRST STEP

GOAL 1: Your child walks independently for 10 feet.
GOAL 2: Your child walks up and down a slight incline.
GOAL 3: Your child walks up and down a steep incline.

REQUIRED SKILL: Your child can walk well with assistance (**34**).

Your child's first steps are a historic moment. With the ability to walk, he discovers a new way to move through space: along his yellow axis, which defines all forward and backward movement. Walking on different surfaces will strengthen his balancing skills, which are the foundation of all movement. Besides, children invariably find the challenge of walking on a mattress to be endless fun.

Before you begin
• Be sure your child is barefoot.
• For Goal 1, clear a flat, matted surface; for Goal 2, set up a slight incline by placing a pillow under one end of a mattress; for Goal 3, put another pillow under the mattress.
• Have available an 11-inch foam or plastic ball.
• Have a partner assist you in spotting the skill.
• Demonstrate walking forward slowly.

1 Sit 3 feet from your coaching partner. Stand your child in front of you, facing your partner. Encourage him to take five or six steps toward your partner and then back to you. Repeat over a span of time.
Repeat at a distance of 5 feet, then 10 feet.

Helpful hints

• Be sure your child does the activity with help before he attempts it on his own.

• A span of time is usually needed in order to learn each step of the skill.

• Say "Walk" and prompt your child to focus forward during the activity.

• If necessary, place your hands lightly on your child's back and rib cage to help him keep his balance.

STEPS TO SKILL MASTERY

1. Child walks a few feet independently.
2. Child walks 10 feet independently.
   Age learned* _____   **Average age learned:** 13 months
3. Child walks 20 feet independently.
4. Child walks up and down a slight incline independently.
   Age learned _____   **Average age learned:** 15 months
5. Child walks up and down a slight incline while holding an 11-inch ball.
6. Child walks up and down a steeper incline independently.
   Age learned _____   **Average age learned:** 24 months
7. Child walks up and down a steep incline while holding an 11-inch ball.

* If you want to keep track of your child's progress, record this age on the appropriate graph in chapter 8.

2 Ask your child to walk up a slight incline.

3 Have your child walk down a slight incline.
When your child can walk up and down a slight incline, repeat on a steeper incline.

40 **THE MAGIC TRICK**

GOAL: Your child tightly squeezes and releases a soft foam ball.

REQUIRED SKILL: Your child can pull a peg from a peg board with his opposing thumb and fingers (**37**).

The Magic Trick develops increased hand strength. It is also a pleasant way to teach your child more about using his hands to control objects. Such awareness sets the foundation for later proficiency in hand-eye coordination.

Before you begin
- Clear a flat, matted surface.
- Have available a 3-inch foam ball.
- Demonstrate squeezing and releasing the ball slowly.

1 Seat your child on the mat or on your lap with his back to you. Give him the ball and ask him to close his hand around it and squeeze as hard as he can. Check if his hand is closed tightly.

Helpful hints
• Say "Close" and "Open" as you encourage your child to focus on the ball in his hand.
• If necessary, place your hand over your child's to help him squeeze the ball.

Let's play
Hold the ball in the palm of your hand and show it to your child. Squeeze it tightly so it disappears. Exclaim "Where's the ball?" Then release your grasp quickly to expose the ball as you say "Here it is!" Give the ball to your child and have him try it. To your little one, this game will seem as wonderful as real magic.

STEPS TO SKILL MASTERY

1. Child can squeeze and release the ball.
   Age learned _____ **Average age learned:** 14 months
2. Child can squeeze and release the ball with either hand.

2 Ask him to open his hand quickly to show the ball. Repeat three times.
Repeat the activity, using the other hand.

41 THE OVERHAND PITCH

GOAL 1: Your child throws a foam ball overhand for 3 feet.
GOAL 2: Your child throws a foam ball overhand for 10 feet.

REQUIRED SKILL: Your child can pull a peg from a peg board with his opposing thumb and fingers (**37**).

The Overhand Pitch promotes hand-eye coordination. Don't be concerned if your child misses the target at first. At this level, the correct motion of the arm is more important than good aim. Your child will discover how to use focus and force to hit a target as he grows better at the skill.

Before you begin

• Clear a flat, matted surface in front of an open doorway.
• Have available a 3-inch foam ball.

Stand or kneel behind your child 2 feet in front of an open doorway. Have him hold the ball in his preferred hand, then raise his hand so that the back of it is resting on or near his shoulder. Place your hand over the hand holding the ball. Encourage him to look through the doorway. Say "Throw" as you help him thrust his arm forward and release the ball toward the target.

Repeat the activity, holding your child's forearm to assist him through the motion. Gradually release your grip so he attempts to throw the ball through the doorway himself.

When he can throw consistently from 3 feet away, repeat the activity with your child standing 5 and then 10 feet from the doorway.

• Demonstrate throwing the ball through the doorway slowly.

Helpful hints
• Be sure your child does the activity with help before he attempts it on his own.
• A span of time is usually needed in order to learn each step of the skill.
• Be sure your child's arm points straight upright to begin the pitch and forward to about a 45-degree angle to release the ball.

STEPS TO SKILL MASTERY
1. Child throws the ball overhand.
2. Child throws the ball overhand through the doorway from 3 feet away.
   Age learned _____   **Average age learned:** 14 months
3. Child throws the ball overhand through the doorway from 3 feet away three times in a row.
4. Child throws the ball overhand through the doorway from 10 feet away.
   Age learned _____   **Average age learned:** 21 months
5. Child throws the ball overhand through the doorway from 10 feet away three times in a row.

42 **SILLY LEGS**

GOAL 1: Your child balances on her right foot with help.
GOAL 2: Your child balances on her left foot with help.

REQUIRED SKILL: Your child can walk up and down a slight incline (**39-2**).

The better a child can balance while standing still, the safer she will be when she is in motion. Always introduce one-foot balancing activities on the preferred leg first. This promotes greater confidence in skill learning, because children tend to have more strength and control on their dominant side.

Before you begin
• Be sure your child is barefoot.
• Clear a flat, matted surface.
• Demonstrate the skill slowly.

Have your child stand with her feet shoulder width apart, and focusing forward. Stand behind her and support her back and rib cage. Encourage her to bend her left knee and raise her left foot slightly off the floor. If necessary, gently lift her leg as shown. Loosen your grip a bit and ask her to hold the right-footed balance for 2 seconds. Assist her back to the starting position.
    Repeat the activity on the other foot.

Let's play

Stand facing your child. Hold her hands at her chest level. Say "Look, I shake a leg!" as you demonstrate gently shaking a leg in front of you. Say *"You* shake a leg!" as you encourage her to shake her opposite leg at the same time. Repeat the game on the other foot.

STEPS TO SKILL MASTERY

1. Child attempts to stand on one foot with help.
2. Child balances on her right foot for 2 seconds with help.
   Age learned _____ **Average age learned:** 16 months
3. Child balances on her left foot for 2 seconds with help.
   Age learned _____ **Average age learned:** 16 months

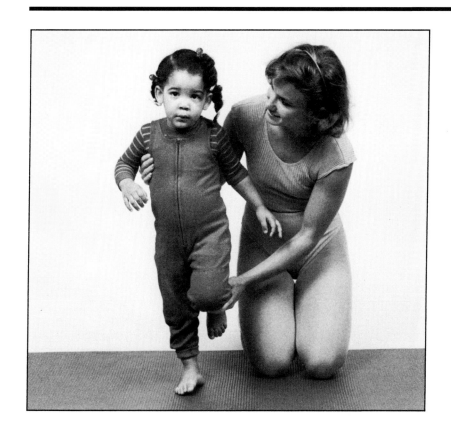

43 UPSTAIRS, DOWNSTAIRS

GOAL 1: Your child walks up and down a 2-inch step with help.
GOAL 2: Your child walks up and down a 2-inch step independently.
GOAL 3: Your child walks up and down ordinary steps independently.

REQUIRED SKILL: Your child can walk up and down a slight incline (**39-2**).

Walking up and down stairs is a major challenge for toddlers. Most children first learn to climb one step at a time, usually leading with the same foot. Only later do they learn to alternate feet, an important advance in bilateral motion. Be sure your child can climb competently and safely on steps scaled to his own size before you let him climb the larger steps ordinarily found in houses.

1 Supporting his back and rib cage securely with your hands, stand your child at the bottom of the small steps and encourage him to focus forward. Say "Step" as you assist him in walking up the steps. *Do not push.* Help your child down the steps.

Before you begin
• Be sure your child is barefoot.
• For Goals 1 and 2, set up a series of steps approximately 2 inches in height using three heavy books, such as two 2-inch-thick encyclopedia volumes and one 4-inch-thick dictionary. Place the books on the floor next to each other lengthwise, with the thicker book in the middle. For Goal 3, use a carpeted stairway.
• Demonstrate stepping up and down slowly.

Helpful hints
• Be sure your child does the activity with help before he attempts it on his own.
• A span of time is usually needed in order to learn each step of the skill.
• See if your child steps up with alternating feet. If not, then help him to step up on the other foot by gently lifting it from the lower leg.
• When assisting, never hold your child's hand above his chest, or you will disturb his center of balance.

2 When he can climb up and down the stairs well with full support, repeat the activity holding his hand to the side at chest level. Over time, gradually release your grip until he can step up and down the shallow stairs independently.
Repeat, using ordinary stairs.

STEPS TO SKILL MASTERY

1. Child walks up and down shallow steps on the same foot with help.
2. Child walks up and down shallow steps on alternating feet with help.
   Age learned _____   **Average age learned:** 16 months
3. Child walks up and down shallow steps on the same foot independently.
4. Child walks up and down shallow steps on alternating feet independently.
   Age learned _____   **Average age learned:** 30 months
5. Child walks up and down ordinary steps on the same foot.
6. Child walks up and down ordinary steps on alternating feet.
   Age learned _____   **Average age learned:** 30 months

44 **ON THE BEAM**

GOAL: Your child stands on a floor beam for 2 seconds.

REQUIRED SKILLS: Your child can balance on one foot for 2 seconds with help (**42**) and can climb up and down steps with help (**43**).

Balancing skills that have become second nature are suddenly put to the test again when a child steps onto the limited surface of a floor beam. Floor beam activities not only strengthen motor control and balance but also build self-confidence as your child discovers he can successfully achieve a goal even under more difficult conditions.

Before you begin
• Place a 4-inch-wide floor beam on a flat, matted surface, and have a toy on hand.
• Be sure your child is barefoot.
• Demonstrate the activity slowly.

1 Have your child stand on the floor facing the middle of the beam. Stand behind him, supporting his back and rib cage with your hands.

Helpful hints
• Be sure your child does the activity with help before he attempts it on his own.
• Have your child focus forward on a toy placed on the floor 4 feet in front of the beam.
• Be sure your child stands on the beam with his feet shoulder width apart.

Let's play
Make an imaginary puddle out of a large piece of colored paper or cloth, and place it underneath one end of the floor beam. Have your child stand on the beam and ask him to see how long he can stay on it before he steps into the puddle. Assist your child if necessary.

2 Help him step onto the beam. Say "Balance" as you release your grip slightly and encourage him to maintain his balance for 2 seconds. Assist him in stepping back down to the starting position.

45 **HANG LOOSE**

GOAL 1: Your child hangs on a bar above her reach for 2 seconds.

GOAL 2: Your child hangs on a bar above her reach for 5 seconds.

REQUIRED SKILLS: Your child can pull to a stand (**26**) and pull a peg from a peg board with her thumb and fingers (**37**).

Physical strength is important to your child's safety, so it is vital not to neglect the development of your toddler's muscular power. By teaching her to support her own body weight, Hang Loose builds hand and arm strength in a safe environment.

Before you begin
• Securely hang a sturdy rod 1 inch in diameter in a doorway at a height 6 inches above your child's reach, or use a jungle gym crossbar at a playground. Be sure there is a soft, flat surface under the bar.

1 Have your child stand with the bar 6 inches in front of her. Ask her to look at the bar and reach her arms toward it. Stand behind her, firmly holding her back and rib cage.

• Demonstrate the activity. Use a doll if you do not have a bar 6 inches above your own height.

Helpful hints

• Be sure your child does the activity with help before she attempts it on her own.
• A span of time is usually needed in order to learn each step of the skill.
• Make sure your child uses a tight overhand grip on the bar. Her arms and legs should hang straight.

STEPS TO SKILL MASTERY

1. Child hangs on a bar 6 inches above her reach for 2 seconds.
   Age learned _____   **Average age learned:** 18 months
2. Child hangs on a bar 6 inches above her reach for 5 seconds.
   Age learned _____   **Average age learned:** 30 months

2 Say "Hold on" as you gently lift your child to the bar. Release your grip somewhat and encourage her to hang on for 2 seconds. Assist her off the bar. Repeat twice.
When your child can easily hang for 2 seconds, ask her to hold on for up to 5 seconds.

46 **CATCH A BALLOON**

GOAL 1: Your child catches a balloon dropped from 2 inches above her reach.

GOAL 2: Your child catches a balloon dropped from 6 inches above her reach.

REQUIRED SKILL: Your child will try to clap a balloon dropped from 2 inches above her reach (**36**).

Good catching skills are fundamental for successful participation in sports. Catch a Balloon is a safe way to develop this basic hand-eye coordination skill. It's also a delightful game because children love to play with balloons.

1 Sit your child securely on your lap with her back against you. Hold a balloon above and slightly forward of her reach. Ask her to look at the balloon and reach for it. Say "Catch" as you release the balloon. Hold her forearms to assist her if necessary.

Before you begin
- Clear a flat, matted surface.
- Have available a 7-inch balloon.
- Demonstrate catching a balloon slowly.

Helpful hint
- A span of time is usually needed in order to learn each step of the skill.

STEPS TO SKILL MASTERY

1. Child catches a balloon dropped from 2 inches above her reach while sitting.
   Age learned _____   **Average age learned:** 18 months
2. Child catches a balloon dropped from 2 inches above her reach while standing.
3. Child catches a balloon dropped from 6 inches above her reach while sitting.
   Age learned _____   **Average age learned:** 30 months
4. Child catches a balloon dropped from 6 inches above her reach while standing.

2 Stand your child on the mat and stand facing her. Hold the balloon above and forward of her reach and repeat the activity.

When your child can easily catch a balloon dropped from 2 inches above her reach, repeat the activity, dropping the balloon from farther away. Gradually increase the distance to 6 inches.

47 **STACK AND BUILD**

GOAL: Your child stacks three toy blocks.

REQUIRED SKILL: Your child can pull a peg from a peg board with his thumb and fingers (**37**).

Stacking blocks develops manual strength as well as precision and teaches your child about spatial relationships between objects. Your child is sure to be pleased with himself as he discovers he can build things and knock them down, too.

Before you begin
• Clear a flat area on the floor.
• Have available three toy blocks.
• Demonstrate stacking the blocks slowly, saying "Carefully" as you do. Then say "Ooops!" as you knock them down.

Seat your child on the floor and place three blocks in front of him. Encourage him to focus on his fingertips grasping each block, and say "Carefully" as he stacks them one on top of the other. When he succeeds, encourage him to knock the tower down. Repeat three times.

Helpful hint

• If necessary, place your hand over your child's to assist him.

STEPS TO SKILL MASTERY

1. Child successfully stacks the blocks.
   Age learned _____   **Average age learned:** 18 months
2. Child successfully stacks the blocks three times in a row.

48 COPYCAT

GOAL 1: Your child demonstrates the basic body positions with help while on her back.

GOAL 2: Your child demonstrates the basic body positions while sitting.

GOAL 3: Your child demonstrates the basic body positions while standing.

REQUIRED SKILL: Your child can walk up and down a slight incline (**39-2**).

The straight, pike, straddle and tuck are basic body positions used in advanced movement skills. Playing Copycat, your child will learn to actively assume these distinct shapes as she strengthens her lower body.

Before you begin
• Clear a flat, matted surface.
• Demonstrate the four positions slowly.

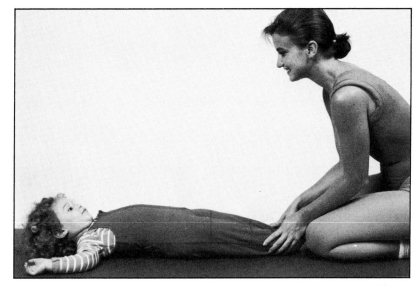

1 Place your child on her back on the mat. Kneeling at her feet, grasp her lower legs and place them straight and together on the mat.

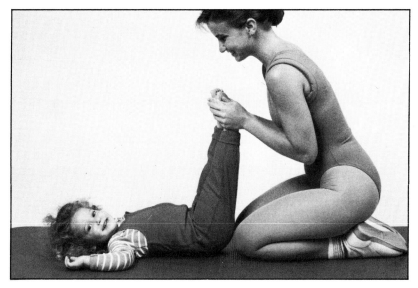

2 Lift her legs up to an *L* position.

Helpful hints
• Be sure your child does the activity with help before she attempts it on her own.
• A span of time is usually needed in order to learn each step of the skill.

Let's play
To practice the four basic body positions, play a game of Simon Says while lying down, sitting and standing.

STEPS TO SKILL MASTERY

1. Child demonstrates the four positions with help while on her back.
   Age learned _____ **Average age learned:** 18 months
2. Child demonstrates the four positions independently while on her back.
3. Child demonstrates the four positions while sitting.
   Age learned _____ **Average age learned:** 20 months
4. Child demonstrates the four positions three times in a row while sitting.
5. Child demonstrates the four positions while standing.
   Age learned _____ **Average age learned:** 30 months
6. Child demonstrates the four positions three times in a row while standing.

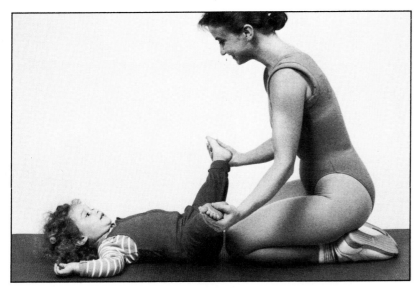

3 Open her legs to a *V* position.

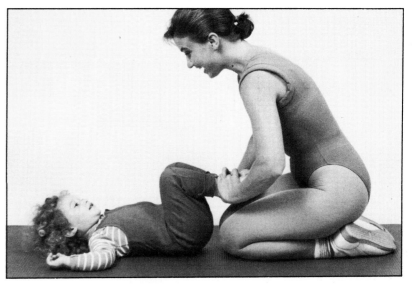

4 Bring her legs together and tuck her knees toward her chest.
Move her legs through the four positions in reverse order. Repeat the activity, gradually releasing your grip until your child can demonstrate the four positions independently.

(continued)

COPYCAT (continued)

5 Have your child lie on the mat with her legs together. Ask her to return to a sit, keeping her legs straight and together in an *L*.

6 Have her open her legs to form a *V*.

8 When your child can easily demonstrate the four positions while sitting, ask her to stand upright with her feet together.

9 Have her bend from the waist and touch the floor with her hands.

7 Have her bring her legs together and tuck her knees toward her chest.
Ask her to do the positions in reverse order.

10 Have her stand upright and spread her legs apart to form a V.

11 Have her bring her feet together, bend her knees, and sit on her heels.
Ask her to do the positions in reverse order.

Before you continue, turn back to the goal listed below. This skill should be learned before you introduce the next exercise.
48/Copycat, Goal 2

49 THE FRONT RUNNER

GOAL 1: Your child runs independently for 10 feet.
GOAL 2: Your child runs up and down a slight incline.

REQUIRED SKILL: Your child can walk up and down a slight incline (**39-2**).

Running challenges a child to maintain coordination and balance while moving swiftly. Toddlers do not run the same way as adults. Their running steps look more like a quick walk, lacking the bounce of a mature runner.

Before you begin
• Be sure your child is barefoot.
• For Goal 1, clear a flat, matted surface; for Goal 2, set up a slightly inclined surface by placing pillows underneath one end of a mattress.

1 Have your child stand on the mat with his feet shoulder width apart. Stand beside him and hold his hand out to the side at chest level. Say "Walk," then "Faster" as you walk forward with him and gradually quicken the pace. Then say "Run" and get him to run with you. Over time, slowly release your grip until he can run independently.
Repeat, running 5 and then 10 feet.

- Have available an 11-inch foam or plastic ball.
- Demonstrate running forward with effort.

Helpful hints

- Be sure your child does the activity with help before he attempts it on his own.
- A span of time is usually needed in order to learn each step of the skill.
- When assisting your child, never pull him by the arm or hold his hand above his chest, or you will disturb his center of balance.
- Encourage him to focus forward as he runs.

> ### STEPS TO SKILL MASTERY
> 1. Child runs 5 feet independently.
> 2. Child runs 10 feet independently.
>   **Age learned** _____   **Average age learned:** 20 months
> 3. Child runs 20 feet independently.
> 4. Child runs up and down a slight incline independently.
>   **Age learned** _____   **Average age learned:** 30 months
> 5. Child runs up and down a slight incline while holding an 11-inch ball.

Before you continue, turn back to the goal listed below. This skill should be learned before you introduce the next exercise.
41/The Overhand Pitch, Goal 2

2 When your child can run well, repeat the activity, having him run down a slight incline.

3 Do the exercise again, this time with your child running up a slight incline.

50 **LOOK AT A BOOK**

GOAL: Your child turns the pages of a book one at a time.

REQUIRED SKILL: Your child can pull a peg from a peg board with his thumb and fingers in opposition (**37**).

Story time is always a special experience between parent and child. It is a chance to share quiet, intimate moments and to expose your child to the world of books, whose words and pictures are a window to learning. Story time is also an excellent opportunity to practice important fine motor skills in a warm and enjoyable atmosphere.

Before you begin
• Be sure the room is well lit.
• Have available a small book with cardboard pages and other picture books of various sizes.

Seat your child securely on your lap with his back against you. Hold a cardboard book open on his lap. Say "Turn the page" as you hold up one page and ask him to grasp it. Make sure his thumb is on one side of the page and his fingers on the other as he turns each page.
Repeat the activity, using different books.

• Demonstrate opening the book and turning the pages slowly.

Helpful hints
• Encourage your child to focus on his fingers as he turns each page.
• If necessary, place your hand over his to help.

Let's play
At story time, seat your child on your lap and place a book with cardboard pages on his lap. Encourage him to hold the book, then ask him to open it and see what is inside. Look at the pictures or read the story. Ask him "What happens next?" as he turns the pages. Assist him if necessary.

STEPS TO SKILL MASTERY

1. Child turns one page at a time.
   Age learned _____   **Average age learned:** 21 months
2. Child turns the pages of various-sized books.

51 PUSH AND PULL

GOAL: Your child pushes and pulls a toy across the floor.

REQUIRED SKILLS: Your child can pull a peg from a peg board with his thumb and fingers (**37**) and can walk independently (**39-1**).

Push and Pull develops your child's sense of accomplishment and command as he discovers he can simultaneously move himself and a large object across the floor by directing his effort in a specific way. Note that pushing is *not* a prerequisite for pulling, or vice versa. Children may develop these skills in either order.

Before you begin
- Clear a flat, bare surface on the floor.
- Have available a push-toy (such as a stroller, doll

1 Stand your child at one end of the room and place the push-toy in his hands. Put your hands over your child's and gently help him push the toy across the room, saying "Push" as you do. Gradually provide less assistance to allow your child to push on his own.
Repeat the activity, using a large empty box in place of the push-toy.

carriage or toy lawn mower) and an empty box that is waist-to-chest high on your child.
• Demonstrate pushing and pulling the toy slowly.

Helpful hint

• As your child pulls the toy, he may actually walk backward or he may turn his body and walk sideways. Although these skills tend to develop later, your child will be able to take a few steps backward or sideways by supporting himself on the toy as he pulls it.

STEPS TO SKILL MASTERY

1. Child pushes a push-toy across the floor.
   Age learned _____   **Average age learned:** 21 months
2. Child pushes a large box across the floor.
3. Child pulls a push-toy across the floor.
   Age learned _____   **Average age learned:** 21 months
4. Child pulls a large box across the floor.

2 Repeat the activity, this time pulling the objects across the floor.

52 **THE OSTRICH STAND**

GOAL 1: Your child balances on her right foot independently for 2 seconds.

GOAL 2: Your child balances on her left foot independently for 2 seconds.

REQUIRED SKILL: Your child can balance on either foot with help (**42**).

The Ostrich Stand teaches endurance as your child tries to maintain a difficult balance. It also develops awareness of the difference in feeling between right and left as your child experiences the greater effort required to balance on one side of her body than on the other.

Before you begin
• Be sure your child is barefoot.
• Clear a flat, matted surface.
• Demonstrate the skill slowly.

Helpful hints
• Be sure your child does the activity with help before she attempts it on her own.

1 Have your child stand with feet shoulder width apart and encourage her to focus forward. Hold her left hand out to her side at chest level, as shown. Say "Stand on one leg" and encourage your child to bend her left knee and raise her foot just off the floor. If necessary, place your left hand on the front of her shin and gently lift her leg. Ask her to hold the right-foot balance for 2 seconds. Assist her back to the starting position.

• A span of time is usually needed in order to learn each step of the skill.
• Introduce the activity on the left leg first if that is your child's dominant side.
• Do not raise your child's hands above chest level to assist her, or you will disturb her center of balance.

Let's play

Stand facing your child and hold her hands at her chest level. Say "Touch toes" as you point your right toe in front of you. Ask your child to extend her left toe forward to touch yours. Repeat three times, then try the game with your other foot.

STEPS TO SKILL MASTERY

1. Child balances on her right foot independently for 2 seconds.
   Age learned _____   **Average age learned:** 23 months
2. Child balances on her right foot independently for 5 seconds.
3. Child balances on her left foot independently for 2 seconds.
   Age learned _____   **Average age learned:** 24 months
4. Child balances on her left foot independently for 5 seconds.

2 Repeat the activity, gradually releasing your grip so your child attempts to balance on her right foot independently.

When your child can balance for 2 seconds on her preferred foot, do the activity on the other foot.

53 **FIRST FLIGHT**

GOAL 1: Your child jumps in place.
GOAL 2: Your child jumps forward.

REQUIRED SKILL: Your child can run well (**49-1**).

Jumping is a completely new way to move through space. With First Flight, your child experiences body control off the ground, laying the foundation for other flight-phase activities such as hopping and skipping.

Before you begin
• Be sure your child is barefoot.
• Clear a flat, matted surface.
• Demonstrate jumping up and down, forward, and backward slowly.

Helpful hints
• Be sure your child does the activity with help before she attempts it on her own.
• Say "Up," "Jump," or "Jump forward" to motivate your child to do the activity.
• Holding her back and rib cage, gently boost your

1 Have your child stand with her knees bent and focusing forward. Kneel behind her, supporting her back and rib cage. Ask her to jump in place as high as she can. If necessary, help her to jump.

2 Have your child take the starting position again. Face her, holding her hands in front of her at chest level. Encourage her to jump in place with you. Gradually release your grip until your child can jump up and down once on her own.

child up if needed, but do not lift or carry her through the activity.

• Never hold your child's hands at shoulder level or higher. Never pull on her arms to lift her.

• Remember: the blue axis runs head to toe and the yellow axis runs front to back.

• In all flight-phase activities, the body moves up and down along the blue axis, so the body is always blue. When you jump forward, the body also moves through yellow space, so we say the movement combines colors—an ability essential to high-level skills.

STEPS TO SKILL MASTERY

1. Child jumps in place once independently.
   Age learned _____   **Average age learned:** 23 months
2. Child jumps forward once independently.
   Age learned _____   **Average age learned:** 29 months
3. Child jumps backward once independently.

Before you continue, turn back to the goals listed below. These skills should be learned before you introduce the next exercise.
52/The Ostrich Stand, Goal 2
39/The First Step, Goal 3

3 From the starting position, support your child's back and rib cage, as shown, and ask her to jump forward as far as she can.

4 Return your child to the starting position. Face her, holding her hands in front of her at chest level. Ask her to jump forward as you jump backward.

Repeat, this time with your child jumping backward.

54 HOT POTATO

GOAL 1: Your child catches a ball rolled from 5 feet away using two hands.

GOAL 2: Your child rolls a ball forward for 5 feet using two hands.

REQUIRED SKILL: Your child can clap her hands together (**31**).

Children are fascinated by balls and other round objects by the way they feel and the way they move. Hot Potato develops hand-eye coordination and manipulative skills, to help ensure that your toddler's first social activities will be fun and successful. Note that children generally learn to catch a ball some time before they learn to roll it.

Before you begin

• Place a 5-foot strip of masking tape on a flat, matted surface.
• Have available a 5-inch foam ball and your child's favorite toy.
• Have a coaching partner assist you.
• Demonstrate the activities slowly with your coaching partner.

1 Seat your child with legs apart on one end of the taped runway, with your partner facing her 5 feet away. Sit behind your child and hold her hands with palms facing each other 10 inches apart.

2 Have your partner roll the ball and help your child clap it between her hands.
Repeat, holding only your child's forearms. Gradually provide less assistance until she catches the ball on her own.

Helpful hints

• Say "Catch" and have your child focus on the ball as you help her catch it.

• Say "Roll" as you help your child push the ball. To help her focus, place a toy 5 feet away between your partner's legs.

Let's play

Turn the ball into a hot potato that you and your child have to roll away as soon as you catch it. When your child is skilled enough to roll and catch on her own, you can sit opposite her and roll the hot potato between you without a coaching partner. Children love this fast-paced game.

STEPS TO SKILL MASTERY

1. Using both hands, child catches a ball rolled from 5 feet away.
   Age learned _____   **Average age learned:** 24 months
2. Using both hands, child catches a ball rolled from 5 feet away three times in a row.
3. Using both hands, child rolls a ball 5 feet.
   Age learned _____   **Average age learned:** 30 months
4. Using both hands, child rolls a ball 5 feet three times in a row.

3 When your child can catch the ball with ease, start with the ball between your child's legs, placing her hands around it, as shown. Help her push the ball toward your partner. Have your partner roll the ball back. Tell your child to catch it and roll it again.

4 Repeat, holding only your child's forearms. Gradually provide less assistance until she rolls the ball on her own.

55 **ZIP, ZIP, ZIP**

GOAL: Your child unzips and zips a zipper.

REQUIRED SKILL: Your child can turn the pages of a cardboard book (**50**).

Zipping requires not only thumb-finger opposition, but the more precise thumb-forefinger opposition. Zipping also adds a challenging constraint to fine motor activity, demanding strict control of the hand in an up-and-down motion. Of course, Zip, Zip, Zip, along with other skills that follow, will come in handy as your child learns to dress and undress herself.

Before you begin
• Clear a flat, matted surface (optional).
• Be sure the room is well lit.

Seat your child on your lap with her back against you or on the mat next to you. Hold the sweater or toy, and encourage your child to focus on her fingers as you place her thumb and forefinger around the zipper tongue. Say "Unzip" and "Zip" each time your child attempts to open and close the zipper.
Repeat the activity on a sweater your child is wearing.

• Have available a 7-inch zipper on a sweater or toy.
• Demonstrate unzipping and zipping slowly.

Helpful hint

• If necessary, keep your fingers over hers to help.

Let's play

Here's a peekaboo game you can play with zippers. Seat your child and give her a zippered sweater or toy. As you unzip it, ask your child "What's behind the zipper?" When it's finally unzipped, pull open the sides and say "Peekaboo!"

STEPS TO SKILL MASTERY

1. Child unzips and zips a 7-inch zipper.
   Age learned _____   **Average age learned:** 24 months
2. Child unzips and zips a 7-inch zipper three times in a row.

56 **LOGGER LEGS**

GOAL 1: Your child steps sideways across a floor beam with help.

GOAL 2: Your child walks forward across a floor beam with help.

REQUIRED SKILLS: Your child can climb steps with help (**43-1**) and can stand on a floor beam (**44**).

Walking sideways is a real challenge for toddlers. It is actually easier for them to sidestep on the restricted surface of the floor beam than across open space, because their path is mapped out for them.

Before you begin
• Place a 4-inch-wide, 8-foot-long floor beam on a flat, matted surface.
• Have a toy available.
• Be sure your child is barefoot.
• Demonstrate the activity slowly.

1 Supporting her back and rib cage, help your child step onto one end of the beam, as shown. Make sure her feet are shoulder width apart and parallel.

2 Help her move her right foot sideways a little, then bring her left foot up to meet it. Proceed in this manner to the end of the beam, then help her off.
Repeat the sidestep activity, standing behind your child and holding her hands to her side at chest level.

Helpful hints

• Be sure your child does the activity with full support before she attempts it with her hands held.
• A span of time is usually needed in order to learn each step of the skill.
• Say "Step slowly" or "Walk slowly" during the activity.
• As your child sidesteps across the beam (steps 1 and 2), have her focus forward on a toy placed 4 feet away; as she walks forward (step 3) have her focus on a toy placed at the opposite end of the beam.
• Never hold your child's hands at shoulder level or higher, or you will disturb her center of balance.
• If your child falls off the beam as she attempts to walk along it, have her get back on at the point where she fell and continue to the end.

Let's play

Pretend the floor beam is a log bridge lying across a big puddle. Have your child mount the beam and ask her to walk across the bridge sideways without falling into the puddle. Try the game walking forward across the bridge. Assist your child as necessary.

3 Help your child walk forward along the beam, supporting her back and rib cage as needed, or stand behind your child and hold her hands to her side at chest level as she steps forward on her right foot and then brings her left foot ahead of it.

STEPS TO SKILL MASTERY

1. Child takes a few sideways steps with her hands held.
2. Child sidesteps the full length of the beam with her hands held.
   Age learned _____   **Average age learned:** 26 months
3. Child takes a few sideways steps independently.
4. Child walks forward a few steps with her hands held.
5. Child walks forward the full length of the beam with her hands held.
   Age learned _____   **Average age learned:** 26 months
6. Child walks forward a few steps independently.

57 **THE TREASURE HUNT**

GOAL: Your child picks up various-sized coins from a flat surface.

REQUIRED SKILL: Your child can unzip and zip a zipper (**55**).

Good hand-eye coordination includes good depth perception. The Treasure Hunt develops dexterity and visual acuity as your child learns to manipulate her hand and fingers to pick up coins of different sizes.

Before you begin

• Clear a flat, matted surface and be sure the room is well lit.
• Have available a quarter, a nickel, a penny and a dime. *Do not leave your child unattended with the coins.*
• Demonstrate picking up each coin slowly.

Helpful hints

• Be sure your child focuses on her fingertips as she picks up each coin.
• If she needs help, keep your fingers over hers.

Seat your child on the mat with her legs apart and place the coins between her legs. Sit behind her and place the thumb and forefinger of her preferred hand around the quarter, saying "Pick it up" as you do. Ask her to pick up the other coins one at a time.
Repeat the activity, using the other hand.

STEPS TO SKILL MASTERY

1. Child picks up various coins with her preferred hand.
   Age learned _____ **Average age learned:** 27 months
2. Child picks up various coins with her other hand.

Before you continue, turn back to the goals listed below. These skills should be learned before you introduce the next exercise.

53/First Flight, Goal 2

43/Upstairs, Downstairs, Goal 2

43/Upstairs, Downstairs, Goal 3

45/Hang Loose, Goal 2

46/Catch a Balloon, Goal 2

48/Copycat, Goal 3

49/The Front Runner, Goal 2

54/Hot Potato, Goal 2

58 **STRONG FINGERS**

GOAL: Your child squeezes open a small plastic clothespin.

REQUIRED SKILL: Your child can pick up various-sized coins from a flat surface (**57**).

This activity tests a child's hand strength and dexterity. It also demonstrates to children that their own actions can cause a reaction from an object. In this case, a clothespin opens and closes as a reward for their effort. This ability to produce a specific reaction through purposeful action builds self-confidence.

Before you begin
• Clear a flat, matted surface and be sure the room is well lit.
• Have available a small plastic clothespin.
• Demonstrate squeezing a clothespin open slowly, holding it 10 inches in front of your child.

Seat your child on the mat. Place her thumb and forefinger on either side of the clothespin and say "Squeeze." Encourage her to focus on her fingertips. If necessary, place your fingers around hers to help. Repeat three times in a row.

STEPS TO SKILL MASTERY
1. Child squeezes open a clothespin.
   Age learned _____   **Average age learned:** 30 months
2. Child squeezes open a clothespin three times in a row.

59 THE STRADDLE HANG

GOAL: Your child hangs on a bar above his reach with his legs in a straddle position.

REQUIRED SKILLS: Your child can hang on a bar in a straight position for 5 seconds (**45**) and can demonstrate the basic body positions (**48**).

The Straddle Hang combines two previously learned activities to create a new one, while developing arm and stomach muscles. Children tend to strengthen their leg muscles naturally through outdoor play, but arm and upper body muscles usually need special attention.

Before you begin

• Securely hang a sturdy rod 1 inch in diameter in a doorway at a height 6 inches above your child's

1 Have your child stand with the bar 6 inches in front of him. Ask him to look at the bar and reach his arms toward it. Stand behind him and hold his back and rib cage firmly.

reach, or use a jungle gym crossbar at a playground. Be sure there is a soft, flat surface under the bar.
• Demonstrate the activity. Use a doll if you do not have a bar 6 inches above your own height.

Helpful hints
• Your child should do the activity with help before he attempts it on his own.
• Be sure your child uses a tight overhand grip on the bar. His arms should hang straight.

2 Say "Hold on" as you gently lift your child to the bar. Say "Straddle" as you release your grip slightly. Tell him to hang on with his legs spread in a *V* for 2 seconds. Repeat twice.

Repeat the activity, encouraging your child to hold the straddle hang position for 5 seconds.

LEARNING TO
HOP, SKIP, LEAP AND SPIN

Between the ages of 2½ and 6, youngsters become increasingly social, learning to play with other children and to participate in structured activities and games, often without you there to supervise. At this stage, physical constitution and skill begin to play a critical role in how your child sees himself and others. Whether he is at the playground with friends or in a preschool program, the Gerard Method will improve his performance and bolster his sense of independence.

The 37 activities in this final stage of the program require more problem solving and mind-body coordination than ever before. Level Three introduces flight-phase skills, such as hopping, skipping and leaping, and rotational skills, such as a forward roll and a jump with a full turn. For the first time, in order to complete a movement, a youngster must rely on how it feels. He can no longer simply see that he has done it correctly. In terms of the Body Color Theory, the child learns to combine colors for the first time as well. A forward roll, for example, is a red body rotation moving forward through yellow space. The ability to combine performance colors demonstrates a high level of problem solving, control and freedom.

Your child will also learn some very important yet practical fine motor skills, such as how to open and close the snaps, buckles and zippers that fasten his clothes and how to hold a pencil and draw basic shapes. In addition, he will develop the strength to support his entire body weight on his arms and the coordination to throw, kick or bat a ball to a target. And he will learn how to fine tune his movement so he can accomplish skills with grace.

After completing Level Three, youngsters are well prepared for virtually any physical task, because no type of movement will be totally unfamiliar to them. More important, they will emerge from the program with a strong self-image and the confidence to meet the many challenges of growing up.

Some special coaching tips for the preschooler's parents

One development at this stage of learning that will greatly change your coaching relationship to your child is that you can talk to him and be understood—and he can talk back. Finally he is able to tell you for himself two very important things: "I don't understand" and "I don't want to." He can also understand your coaching commands well enough to relate them to new movement experiences.

This is the stage, too, when your child wants to be just like you—or anyone else who catches his fancy—and he will naturally imitate behavior. In addition, it is also a very imaginative phase of life, when your child enjoys being things also. In "Let's Play" activities, he will love to imagine puddles and trees or pretend to be an ostrich or feel like a cloud.

Always follow the step-by-step instructions for each activity, and refer to the checklist on page 19 for general coaching guidelines. Remember that, at this level especially, many skills have multiple goals, which means your child may require a period of time to learn each step before going on to the next. As you go along, you and your child will enjoy greater success if you follow these additional tips as well:

• Performance is important in Level Three. In Level Two, skill learning emphasized getting down the basic motions only. Now, however, your child is ready for the challenge of adding correct focus, pointed toes and straight arms and legs, to tune up his performance.

Keep in mind that while correct focus improves the "look" of a skill, it is also essential to safety, especially when performing flight-phase and rotation skills.

• Your approval is very important to your child at this age, and more than ever your encouragement and support as he attempts new skills are vital to his developing sense of self. He judges other children by their physical capabilities, and he understands that this is how they view him, too. The criticized child may believe that his lack of ability somehow makes him a lesser person.

• Emphasize activities in those areas where he needs extra help. Even if you have not been using the performance charts all the way through, you should still have a pretty good sense of your child's physical strengths and weaknesses by the time he is 3 or 4. To ensure well-rounded skill development, it's important to give your child extra opportunities to learn those skills which he finds the hardest to do. Don't forget to let him get plenty of exercise doing what he likes and does well, too—or you may discourage his interest in movement altogether.

• Introduce the colors of movement to your child as soon as he is old enough to learn them. The Body Color Theory describes all motion in terms of three axes that run through the body: the blue axis runs from head to toe, the yellow axis runs from front to back, and the red axis runs from side to side. You can move either along an axis (this is called a translation) or around an axis (called a rotation). No matter how you move, the axes remain constant in the positions described.

60 WHAT'S MY COLOR?

GOAL: Your child learns to identify the blue, yellow and red axes of movement.

REQUIRED SKILLS: Your child can run well (**49**) and can recognize colors.

This activity is slightly different from the others in the book, because it is concerned with teaching a concept rather than a particular motor skill. Its purpose is to introduce your child to her blue, yellow and red axes as an aid to learning more complex movements. At 30 to 36 months, your youngster is mature enough to understand and play the game of moving on make-believe poles that run through the body. Although she may take some weeks to grasp the idea completely, later on the colors will make skill learning easier and more fun to do.

1 Tell your child that she has an invisible pole that runs through her body from head to toe. Grab your imaginary blue axis and have your child grab hers, as shown. Say "You can move up and down along your blue pole," as you pretend to pull yourself up and down the axis by bending and straightening your legs.

2 Say "You can move around your blue pole, too," as you twist your body to the left and right. Say "These are blue movements," then ask your child to show you two ways she can be blue. Assist her if necessary.

Before you begin
• Clear a flat, matted surface.

Helpful hints
• As you introduce each axis, say, in step 1, "The color of this pole is blue, and you can do two things on this pole." In step 3, say "The color of this pole is yellow, and you can also do two things on this pole. In step 5, say "The color of this pole is red, and you can do two things on this pole, too."
• As you demonstrate the axes, encourage your child to imitate each movement.
• If you're a good mime, use your hands to rotate the imaginary pole in the same direction as your body as you demonstrate turning on each axis (steps 2, 4 and 6).

Let's play
Play Freeze or Statues with your child when she begins to learn the colors. As she moves about in play, shout "Stop!" or "Freeze!" and then ask her to name the color of her movement.

3 Tell your child that she has another invisible pole, which runs through her body from front to back. Grab your imaginary yellow axis and have your child grab hers, as shown. Say "You can move forward and backward along your yellow pole," as you demonstrate stepping forward and backward along the yellow axis.

(continued)

WHAT'S MY COLOR? *(continued)*

4 Say "You can move around your yellow pole, too," as you bend your body sideward to the left and right. Say "These are yellow movements," then ask your child to show you two ways she can be yellow. Assist her if necessary.

5 Tell your child that she has another invisible pole, one that runs through her body from side to side. Grab your imaginary red axis and have your child grab hers, as shown. Say "You can move side to side along your red pole," as you demonstrate stepping from right to left and left to right.

6 Say "You can move around your red pole, too," as you bend forward and backward at the waist. Say "These are red movements," then ask your child to show you two ways she can be red. Assist her if necessary.

STEPS TO SKILL MASTERY

1. Your child imitates moving along and around each axis with help.
2. Your child demonstrates moving along and around each axis without help.
3. Your child knows the colors of various movements.

Age learned* _____   **Average age learned:** 30 months

* If you want to keep track of your child's progress, record this date on the appropriate graph in chapter 8.

61 ON A ROLL

GOAL: Your child does a forward roll on his red axis.

REQUIRED SKILL: Your child can perform the four body positions (48).

When the body is rolling or spinning, the visual sense is not fast enough to provide the information necessary for body control. Rotation skills, like On a Roll, develop "muscle sense," the ability to control movement by how it feels rather than by how it looks.

Before you begin
• Set up a padded incline and clear a flat, matted surface. You can place a couple of pillows underneath one end of a mattress to make the incline.
• Be sure your child is barefoot.

1 Have your child stand at the top of the incline, facing downhill. Ask him to bend at the waist, with his hands and feet flat on the floor (pike position). Place your hands on his hips, as shown.

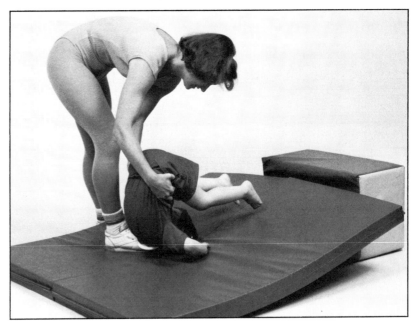

2 Ask your child to look down at his belly and push off with his toes.

• Demonstrate rolling forward slowly yourself or use a doll.

Helpful hint
• Be sure your child does the activity with help before he attempts it on his own.

STEPS TO SKILL MASTERY

1. Child rolls forward down an incline.
2. Child rolls forward on a flat surface.
   Age learned _____   **Average age learned:** 30 months

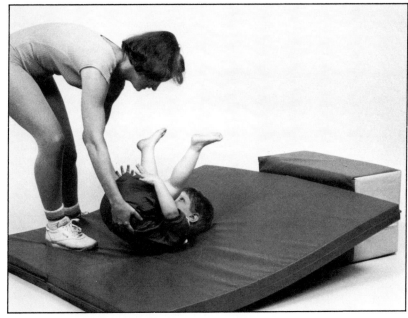

3 Say "Roll forward" as you gently pull forward on his hips. Gradually release your grip so he attempts to roll on his own.

Repeat the activity on a flat surface.

62 **DOT TO DOT**

GOAL 1: Your child draws a 6-inch horizontal line.
GOAL 2: Your child draws a 6-inch vertical line.

REQUIRED SKILL: Your child can unzip and zip a zipper (**55**).

Your child has already learned to grasp, manipulate and communicate things with his hands. With Dot to Dot he discovers he can create with them. In this activity your child learns how to hold a pencil properly between his fingers and how to draw a line—the foundations for good writing skills.

Before you begin
• Set up a chair and table suited to your child's height. Be sure the room is well lit.
• Have available a pencil or crayon and drawing paper.
• Demonstrate the skill slowly.

1 Draw two dots side by side 6 inches apart on a sheet of paper and place it in front of your seated child. Put the pencil or crayon in your child's preferred hand, placing his thumb, forefinger and middle finger as shown. With your hands over his, place the pencil point on the left-hand dot on the paper. Ask him to look at the point, then say "Draw" as you move his hand to the right to connect the dots. Draw two more dots and repeat.

Repeat the activity, holding your child's forearm. Gradually release your grip to enable your child to try the skill on his own.

When your child can draw a horizontal line, go to step 2.

STEPS TO SKILL MASTERY

1. Child draws a 6-inch horizontal line by connecting two dots.
   Age learned _____ **Average age learned:** 30 months
2. Child draws a 6-inch horizontal line without dots.
3. Child draws a 6-inch vertical line by connecting two dots.
   Age learned _____ **Average age learned:** 36 months
4. Child draws a 6-inch vertical line without dots.

2 Repeat the activity, drawing 6-inch vertical lines. Connect the dots top to bottom.

63 MARCHES AND MARATHONS

GOAL 1: Your child marches along his blue, yellow and red axes.

GOAL 2: Your child jogs along his blue, yellow and red axes.

REQUIRED SKILLS: Your child can walk (**39**) and run well (**49**).

In Marches and Marathons, your child learns to take two familiar skills, walking and running, and perform them in various new ways that are fun as well as challenging. Marching blue is walking in place and jogging blue is marching quickly in place. This is the first skill that introduces a movement on all three axes.

Before you begin
• Clear a flat, matted surface. Place strips of yellow and red tape on the floor in a +, with the yellow pointing front to back and the red going from side to

Have your child stand on the blue sticker, facing forward along the yellow strip of tape. Stand directly in front of him with your back toward him. Ask him to focus on you and play follow the leader. Step in place slowly, then double time. Step forward and backward slowly, then double time. Step several times to the right and back to the left, first slowly, then double time.

Repeat the activity, having your child be the leader.

When your child can march well, repeat the activity, jogging on the blue, yellow and red axes.

side. Put a blue sticker where the pieces of tape intersect.
• Be sure your child is barefoot.
• Demonstrate the activity slowly.

Helpful hints
• A span of time is usually needed in order to learn each step of the skill.
• Say "March blue! March yellow! March red!" and "Jog blue! Jog yellow! Jog red! as you march and jog on the different axes. Say "Slowly" and "Quickly" as you alternate the pace of the movements.

• Remember: the blue axis runs head to toe, the yellow axis runs front to back, and the red axis runs side to side.

Let's play
Play a game of Simon Says with your child. Give a series of commands, such as: "Simon says jog blue! Simon says jog red! Simon says march red! Simon says march yellow! Simon says march faster! Slower!"

STEPS TO SKILL MASTERY
1. Child marches along his blue, yellow and red axes.
   Age learned _____   **Average age learned:** 30 months
2. Child marches double time along his blue, yellow and red axes.
3. Child jogs along his blue, yellow and red axes.
   Age learned _____   **Average age learned:** 42 months
4. Child jogs double time along his blue, yellow and red axes.

64 SQUASH THE BUGS

GOAL 1: Your child jumps in place starting on one foot and landing on both.
GOAL 2: Your child jumps forward starting on one foot and landing on both.
GOAL 3: Your child jumps sideways starting on one foot and landing on both.

REQUIRED SKILLS: Your child can balance on one foot (**52**) and can jump once on her blue and yellow axes (**53**).

Squash the Bugs builds upon earlier balancing, flight-phase and spatial skills in an exercise that promotes agility and coordination. Hopping from one foot to both feet, a familiar activity in Hopscotch, is known as an *assemblé*.

Before you begin
• Be sure your child is barefoot.
• Clear a flat, matted surface. Following the diagram, place colored stickers on the mat. *B*'s represent blue stickers, *Y*'s yellow and *R*'s red.
• Demonstrate the activity slowly.

Helpful hints
• Be sure your child does the activity with help before she attempts it on her own.

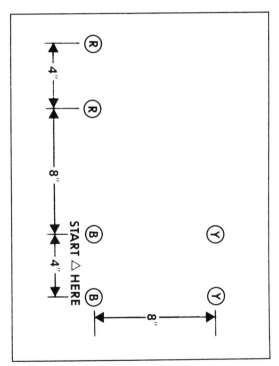

1 Have your child stand with her right foot on the X with her knee bent. Support her back and rib cage as shown.

2 Say "Jump from one to two on blue" as you assist her in reaching both feet to the blue stickers.
Repeat the activity, standing beside your child and holding her hand. Do the assemblé together.

• A span of time is usually needed in order to learn each step of the skill.

• If necessary, lift your child up slightly and tell her, "Feet together." Make sure she focuses forward at all times.

• Remember: the blue axis runs head to toe, the yellow axis runs front to back, and the red axis runs side to side.

Let's play

Play a game of Squash the Bugs with your child. Holding your child's hand, have her assume the starting position for the skill. Call "Squash the blue bugs! Squash the yellow bugs! Squash the red bugs!" as you practice the skill together.

STEPS TO SKILL MASTERY

1. Child jumps in place from one foot to two feet.
   Age learned _____   **Average age learned:** 30 months
2. Child jumps in place from one foot to two feet three times in a row.
3. Child jumps forward from one foot to two feet.
   Age learned _____   **Average age learned:** 30 months
4. Child jumps forward from one foot to two feet three times in a row.
5. Child jumps sideways from one foot to two feet.
   Age learned _____   **Average age learned:** 54 months
6. Child jumps sideways from one foot to two feet three times in a row.

---

3 Assume the starting position again. Say "Jump from one to two on yellow" as you assist her in reaching both feet to the yellow stickers 8 inches forward.

Repeat the activity, standing to the left of your child and holding her hand. Do the assemblé together.

When your child can do this well, go to step 4.

4 Return to the starting position. Say "Jump from one to two on red" as you assist her in reaching both feet to the red stickers 8 inches to the left.

Repeat the activity, standing to the left of your child and holding her hand. Do the assemblé together.

65 REACH FOR THE STARS

GOAL: Your child balances on the balls of his feet for 2 seconds.

REQUIRED SKILL: Your child can balance on one leg for 2 seconds **(52)**.

Your child has come a long way since the days when standing upright was still a precarious business, and he will enjoy the challenge to his secure sense of balance when he tries standing on tiptoe. This skill teaches him to become more aware of his center of gravity and develops ankle and leg strength, too.

Before you begin
• Clear a flat, matted surface.
• Be sure your child is barefoot.
• Have a toy available.
• Demonstrate the activity slowly.

1 Have your child stand with his feet shoulder width apart. Kneel behind him and support his back and rib cage. Encourage him to rock back and forth on his feet, then tell him to stop and balance on the balls of his feet and hold that balance for 2 seconds.

Helpful hints
• Say "Rock" and "On tiptoe" to encourage your child to stand on his toes.
• Have your child focus forward on a toy placed 4 feet away.

Let's play
Cut out a paper star, or use a ball or other object, and hold it 8 to 10 inches above and slightly in front of your child's head. Ask him to stand on tiptoe and reach for the star.

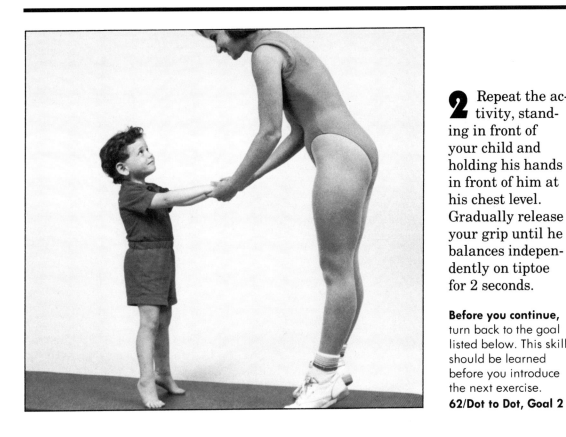

2 Repeat the activity, standing in front of your child and holding his hands in front of him at his chest level. Gradually release your grip until he balances independently on tiptoe for 2 seconds.

Before you continue, turn back to the goal listed below. This skill should be learned before you introduce the next exercise.
62/Dot to Dot, Goal 2

66 HIGH NOON BALLOON

GOAL: Your child catches a balloon dropped from 12 inches above his reach.

REQUIRED SKILL: Your child can catch a balloon dropped from 6 inches above his reach (**46-2**).

High Noon Balloon is an advanced progression of the balloon-catching activity in Level Two. This enjoyable exercise develops important hand-eye co-ordination skills that enable a child to react effectively and safely to moving objects.

Before you begin

• Clear a flat, matted surface.
• Have available a 7-inch balloon.
• Demonstrate catching a balloon slowly.

1 Have your child stand facing you. Hold a balloon 12 inches above and slightly in front of him. Ask him to look at the balloon and reach for it. Say "Catch" as you drop the balloon. Repeat three times.

STEPS TO SKILL MASTERY

1. Child catches a balloon dropped from 12 inches above his reach.
    Age learned _____   **Average age learned:** 36 months
2. Child catches a balloon tossed from 12 inches away.

2 Repeat the activity, tossing the balloon to your child from 12 inches away.

67 THROUGH THE DOOR

GOAL: Your child throws a ball underhand for 6 feet.

REQUIRED SKILL: Your child can throw a ball overhand for 10 feet (**53-2**).

Through the Door strengthens hand-eye coordination. The ability to synchronize arm and hand movements to successfully toss a ball is called a sequencing skill. Motor sequencing fosters an understanding of order, which is critical for reading development.

Before you begin
• Have available a 3-inch foam ball.
• Demonstrate slowly throwing underhand at the target.

1 Have your child stand 6 feet in front of an open doorway with his arms at his sides. Standing behind him, grasp the back of his preferred hand and pull it straight back.

2 Say "Throw" as you swing your child's hand forward. *Release your grip and ask your child to swing his arm back and forth several times until he can do it consistently by himself.*

Helpful hints

• Be sure your child's arm points straight down to start, is drawn back about 70 degrees to begin the throw (step 1), and swings forward to the same angle when he releases the ball (step 2), like the pendulum of a clock.

• Be sure your child focuses on the target at all times.

• Be sure your child swings his arm back and forth in a straight line. It should not cross in front of his body.

3 Offer your child the ball and ask him to throw it through the doorway using the arm motion in step 2. Assist him if necessary. Repeat three times.

68 BUTTON UP

GOAL: Your child unbuttons and buttons a 1-inch button.

REQUIRED SKILL: Your child can unzip and zip a zipper (**55**).

Button Up is a skill that requires the use of both hands simultaneously: one to hold the buttonhole steady and the other to manipulate the button. Learning to use one hand for strength and the other for dexterity develops important bilateral skills.

Before you begin
• Be sure the room is well lit.
• Have available a 1-inch round button on a sweater or jacket.
• Demonstrate unbuttoning and buttoning slowly, holding the button 10 inches in front of your child.

Helpful hints
• Encourage your child to focus on his fingertips during the activity.
• If necessary, help him by keeping your fingers over his.

Seat your child on your lap. Place the thumb and forefinger of his preferred hand on the edge of the button and the thumb and forefinger of his other hand on the edge of the cloth. Say "Unbutton" and "Button" each time your child attempts or achieves the goal.
Repeat the activity on a sweater your child is wearing.

STEPS TO SKILL MASTERY
1. Child unbuttons and buttons a 1-inch button on a sweater.
   Age learned _____   **Average age learned:** 36 months
2. Child unbuttons and buttons a 1-inch button on a sweater he has on.

69 **BUCKLE UP**

GOAL: Your child unfastens and fastens a buckle.

REQUIRED SKILL: Your child can pick up various coins (**57**).

Like buttoning, buckling requires the use of both hands at the same time. Buckle Up also stimulates awareness of important spatial concepts as your child learns to maneuver objects in and out, over and under, up and down.

Before you begin
• Be sure the room is well lit.
• Have available a large buckle on a soft doll, on a shoe or on other clothing.
• Demonstrate unbuckling and buckling slowly, holding the buckle 10 inches in front of your child.

Helpful hints
• Encourage your child to focus on his fingertips during the activity.
• If necessary, keep your fingers over his to help.

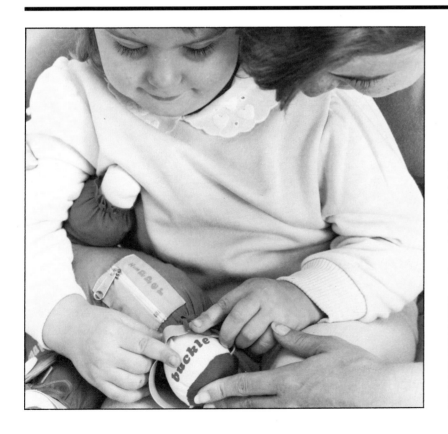

Seat your child on your lap and put the buckle on his lap. Place the thumb and forefinger of his preferred hand on the edge of the buckle, and the thumb and forefinger of his other hand on the strap. Say "Unbuckle" and "Buckle" each time your child attempts or achieves the goal.
Repeat the activity, using a buckle on a shoe or other clothing your child is wearing.

STEPS TO SKILL MASTERY
1. Child unfastens and fastens a buckle.
   Age learned _____   **Average age learned:** 36 months
2. Child unbuckles and buckles a shoe or other clothing he has on.

70 **BOUNCING BALLS**

GOAL 1: Your child catches a ball bounced from 6 feet away.

GOAL 2: Your child bounces and catches a ball with two hands three times in a row.

REQUIRED SKILL: Your child can catch a balloon dropped from 12 inches above his reach (**66**).

Balls move in very predictable ways and their predictability makes them great fun to bounce, throw, catch and chase—and as far as your kid is concerned, that's what's important. While she's having a grand time playing, she's also learning intuitively about the useful physical principles of force, action and reaction, flight and rhythm that govern the movements of a bouncing ball.

Before you begin
• Clear a flat surface.

1 Have your child stand with her feet shoulder width apart. Stand behind her, holding her hands 12 inches apart. Have your partner stand 6 feet away and bounce the ball to your child. Say "Catch" as you help her grasp the bouncing ball. Repeat the exercise, holding your child's forearms, then gradually release your grip as your child becomes more proficient.

Repeat the activity, bouncing the ball from 10 feet away. When she can catch the ball on her own, go on to step 2.

• Have available a 9- or 11-inch rubber ball.
• Have a coaching partner assist you.
• Demonstrate the activities slowly and with effort.

Helpful hints

• Be sure your child does the activity with help before she attempts it on her own.
• A span of time is usually needed in order to learn each step of the skill.
• Be sure your child focuses on the ball.

STEPS TO SKILL MASTERY

1. Child catches a ball bounced from 6 feet away.
   Age learned _____   **Average age learned:** 36 months
2. Child catches a ball bounced from 10 feet away.
3. Child bounces and catches a ball three times in a row.
   Age learned _____   **Average age learned:** 48 months
4. Child bounces and catches a ball five times in a row.

2 This time, have your child hold the ball in her hands at waist level. Say "Bounce" as you help her push the ball directly downward. Say "Catch" as you help her grasp it between her hands again. Repeat the exercise, holding your child's forearms, then gradually release your grip to allow her to attempt to bounce and catch the ball on her own.

Before you continue, turn back to the goal listed below. This skill should be learned before you introduce the next exercise.
63/Marches and Marathons, Goal 2

71 **THE NOSE BOP**

GOAL: Your child does five modified push-ups.

REQUIRED SKILL: Your child can hang on a bar in a straddle position for 5 seconds (**59**).

Muscle power, or strength, enables a child to control her movements and is a basic building block for balancing and coordination skills. In The Nose Bop, your child must raise and lower her body, supporting her weight on her arms while making an effort to keep her legs still and her hips and back straight.

Before you begin
• Clear a flat, matted surface.
• Have available a colored sticker.

1 Have your child get on her hands and knees on the mat. Ask her to walk her hands forward about three steps, until her hips and back are straight. Be sure her hands and elbows are straight.

• Demonstrate the activity slowly. A modified push-up is done on bent knees rather than with the legs fully extended.

Helpful hints
• If necessary, gently support your child's back and rib cage.
• Be sure your child's hips are straight throughout the skill.

STEPS TO SKILL MASTERY

1. Child does five modified push-ups.
   Age learned _____   **Average age learned:** 42 months
2. Child does ten modified push-ups.

2 Place a sticker on the mat between your child's hands and ask her to focus on it. Say "Bop!" and encourage her to lower her body to touch the sticker with her nose. Then say "Push up" and have her push her body back up with her arms. Repeat five times in a row.

72 **LONG AND SHORT**

GOAL: Your child hangs on a bar above his reach with his legs in a tuck position.

REQUIRED SKILLS: Your child can demonstrate the basic body positions (**48**) and can hang on a bar in a straddle position for 5 seconds (**59**).

Long and Short promotes a greater awareness of the role of effort in successfully achieving a skill. Like the earlier hanging activities, this one also develops increased arm and stomach strength.

Before you begin

• Securely hang a sturdy rod 1 inch in diameter in a doorway at a height 6 inches above your child's reach, or use a jungle gym crossbar at a playground. Be sure there is a soft, flat surface under the bar. Do not try this activity on a concrete playground.

1 Have your child stand with the bar 6 inches in front of him. Ask him to look at the bar and reach his arms toward it. Say "Hold on" as you gently lift him up to the bar in a straight-hang position, as shown.

• Demonstrate the activity slowly. Use a doll if you do not have a bar 6 inches above your own height.

Helpful hints

• Be sure your child does the activity with help before he attempts it on his own.
• Be sure your child uses a tight overhand grip on the bar. His arms should hang straight.

Let's play

The "long and short" of this game is simply to have your child alternate between the straight and tuck positions while hanging on the bar. Have your child respond to your commands: "Short" and "Long," or "Tuck" and "Stretch."

STEPS TO SKILL MASTERY

1. Child hangs on a bar 6 inches above his reach with legs tucked for 5 seconds.
   Age learned _____   **Average age learned:** 42 months
2. Child hangs with legs tucked for 10 seconds.

2 Say "Tuck" as you release your grip, and encourage him to hang in a tuck position and count to five. If necessary, grasp the back of his lower thighs and gently lift his knees to his chest to assist. Help him off the bar.

Repeat the activity, telling your child to hold the tuck-hang position for 10 seconds.

73 SNAP IT

GOAL: Your child unfastens and fastens a snap.

REQUIRED SKILL: Your child can unzip and zip a zipper (**55**).

Snapping is a skill that requires strength and a high level of dexterity in both hands at the same time. Snap It requires more precision than buttoning or zipping, but once your child gets the hang of it, there'll be no keeping her clothes on!

Before you begin
• Be sure the room is well lit.
• Have available a ¼-inch snap on a stuffed doll and a snap on your child's clothing.
• Demonstrate unsnapping and snapping slowly, holding the snap 10 inches in front of your child.

Helpful hints
• Encourage your child to focus on her fingertips during the activity.
• If necessary, keep your fingers over hers to help.

Seat your child in front of you and put the snap on her lap. Place the snap top in her preferred hand, with her forefinger on top and her thumb on the bottom edge. Place the edge of the snap bottom between the thumb and forefinger of her other hand. Say "Unsnap" and "Snap" each time your child attempts or achieves the goal.

Repeat the activity, using a snap on a piece of clothing your child is wearing.

STEPS TO SKILL MASTERY

1. Child unfastens and fastens a snap.
   Age learned _____   **Average age learned:** 42 months
2. Child unfastens and fastens a snap on clothing she is wearing.

74 LACE IT UP

GOAL: Your child laces a sequence of holes.

REQUIRED SKILL: Your child can pick up various coins (**57**).

Lacing is a complex activity requiring hand strength and dexterity, as well as a highly developed spatial awareness. Successfully combining skills promotes a positive sense of self through achievement.

Before you begin
• Be sure the room is well lit.
• Have available two items for lacing, one with large holes and another with smaller holes, and two laces, one thicker than the other, to fit the holes. Be sure each lace has a stiff end and a knotted end.
• Demonstrate the skill slowly, holding the item to be laced in one hand and lacing with the other hand.

Helpful hints
• If necessary, help her by keeping your fingers over hers.

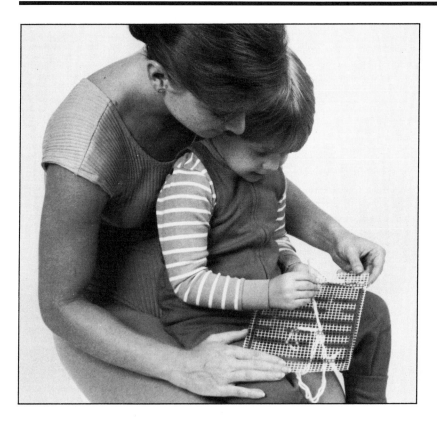

Seat your child with her legs apart and sit behind her. Help her hold the large-holed lacing in one hand. Push the stiff end of the thicker lace up and just through the first hole, then place it between the thumb and forefinger of her preferred hand. Help her pull the lace the rest of the way through the first hole, then push the lace down through the next hole. Encourage her to lace the holes in sequence. Allow your child to try it on her own, holding the lace in her preferred hand and the lacing in the other.

Repeat the activity, lacing the small-holed item with the thinner lace.

STEPS TO SKILL MASTERY
1. Child pushes and pulls a lace through one hole.
2. Child laces a large-holed item by following a sequence of holes.
   Age learned _____   **Average age learned:** 42 months
3. Child laces large and small holes in sequence.

Before you continue, turn back to the goal listed below. This skill should be learned before you introduce the next exercise.
70/Bouncing Balls, Goal 2

75 THE TIGHTROPE WALKER

GOAL 1: Your child walks sideways along a floor beam independently.

GOAL 2: Your child walks forward along a floor beam independently.

REQUIRED SKILLS: Your child can walk sideways and forward along a floor beam with help (**56**) and can balance on tiptoe (**65**).

The Tightrope Walker teaches the importance of balance while in motion and stimulates foot-eye coordination and spatial awareness. The ability to control movement on a limited surface enhances a child's overall sense of physical mastery.

Before you begin
• Place a 4-inch-wide, 8-foot-long floor beam on a flat, matted surface.
• Have a toy available.
• Be sure your child is barefoot.
• Demonstrate the activity slowly.

1 Have your child step onto the left end of the beam, as shown, with her feet shoulder width apart and parallel, her arms out to the side at chest level. Standing slightly behind your child and to one side, hold her hand as she moves her right foot sideways, then brings her left foot over to meet it. Gradually release your grasp as she finds her balance and begins to sidestep independently.

Repeat, having your child step sideways along the beam on tiptoe.

Helpful hints

• Be sure your child does the activity with help before she attempts it on her own.

• Say "Step slowly" or "Walk slowly" during the activity.

• As your child sidesteps along the beam (step 1), have her focus forward on a toy placed 4 feet away; as she walks forward (step 2), have her focus on a toy placed at the opposite end of the beam.

• Never hold your child's hands at shoulder level or higher, or you will disturb her center of balance.

• If your child falls off the beam as she attempts to walk along it, have her get back on at the point where she fell and continue to the end.

Let's play

This is the age when children love to pretend. Ask your child to imagine she is a famous circus performer. Have her mount the beam and walk slowly along it sideways, as if she were walking on a tight-rope high above the center ring. Pretend you are the ringmaster and describe her daring feat as you encourage her to get to the other side. Have her go back along the tightrope, walking forward this time. Assist her as necessary.

2 Help your child onto the beam. Ask her to walk forward. If necessary, hold her hands at chest level. Gradually release your grasp as she finds her balance and begins to walk forward independently.

Repeat, having your child step forward along the beam on tiptoe.

STEPS TO SKILL MASTERY

1. Child walks sideways along the floor beam independently.
   Age learned _____   **Average age learned:** 48 months
2. Child walks sideways along the floor beam on tiptoe.
3. Child walks forward along the floor beam independently.
   Age learned _____   **Average age learned:** 48 months
4. Child walks forward along the floor beam on tiptoe.

76 THE COLORFUL KANGAROO

GOAL 1: Your child jumps in place three times in a row.
GOAL 2: Your child jumps forward and backward three times in a row.
GOAL 3: Your child jumps sideways three times in a row.

REQUIRED SKILL: Your child can jump once on her blue and yellow axes (**53**).

There is generally a long span of time between the age at which a child first learns to jump and that at which she is able to jump many times in a row. To jump up and down once, a child needs to control the force and direction of her movement in relationship to the ground only. Repeated jumping is more complex, because it requires a child to react not only to her stationary surroundings but to her own movement as well. Repeated jumping also stimulates rhythm, which is vital to agility and coordination.

Before you begin
• Be sure your child is barefoot.

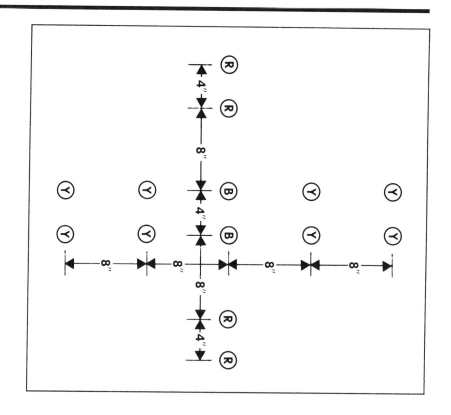

• Clear a flat, matted surface. Following the diagram, place colored stickers on the mat. *B*'s represent blue stickers, *Y*'s yellow and *R*'s red.
• Demonstrate the activity slowly.

Helpful hints
• Be sure your child does the activity with help before she attempts it on her own.
• Remember: the blue axis runs head to toe, the yellow axis runs front to back, and the red axis runs side to side.
• Ask your child to focus forward throughout the activity.

• Give her a boost if needed, but don't lift her off the ground.

Let's play
Play a game of Colorful Kangaroo with your child. Hold her hands and practice jumping in different directions. Have her jump backward as you jump forward, and vice versa. Have her jump to the left as you jump to the right so you jump sideways together, then switch directions. Have your child jump to one side while you jump to the other. You can also play a new game of Colorful Kangaroo Says.

1 Have your child stand on the blue stickers with her knees bent. Support her back and rib cage as shown.

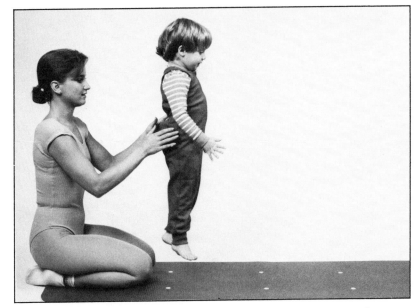

2 Say "Jump blue" as you assist her in jumping in place as high as she can three times in a row.
Repeat the activity, standing in front of your child, holding her hands and jumping in place together.

(continued)

THE COLORFUL KANGAROO *(continued)*

3 Assume the starting position again. Say "Jump forward yellow" as you assist your child in jumping forward to the yellow stickers three times in a row.

Repeat, standing in front of your child and holding her hands. Jump back and forth with her.

4 Return to the starting position. Say "Jump red" as you assist your child in jumping sideways to the red stickers on the right. Repeat three times.

Repeat, standing in front of your child, holding her hands and jumping sideways together. Have her jump right as you jump left.

Repeat the activity on the other side.

STEPS TO SKILL MASTERY

1. Child jumps in place three times in a row.
   Age learned _____   **Average age learned:** 48 months
2. Child jumps in place eight times in a row.
3. Child jumps forward and backward three times in a row.
   Age learned _____   **Average age learned:** 48 months
4. Child jumps forward and backward eight times in a row.
5. Child jumps to the right and left three times in a row.
   Age learned _____   **Average age learned:** 48 months
6. Child jumps to the right and left eight times in a row.

77 THE BUNNY HOP

GOAL 1: Your child hops in place on one foot three times in a row.

GOAL 2: Your child hops forward and backward on one foot three times in a row.

GOAL 3: Your child hops sideways on one foot three times in a row.

REQUIRED SKILL: Your child can jump forward from one foot to both feet (**64-2**).

Flight-phase skills always include a takeoff and a landing, and develop a child's sense of height and reach. In The Bunny Hop, the child takes off from one foot and lands on the same foot. This complex motor activity combines one-foot balancing with jumping skills, creating a new movement. This process of skill building improves a child's problem-solving capacity, which is important when she is on her own in the playground.

Before you begin

• Be sure your child is barefoot.

• Clear a flat, matted surface. Follow the diagram and place stickers on the mat. *B, R* and *Y* represent blue, red and yellow stickers.

• Demonstrate the activity slowly.

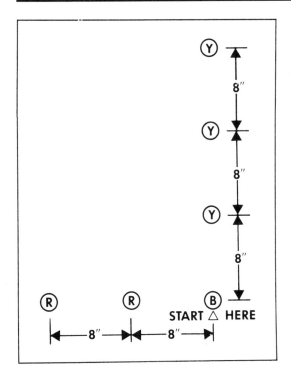

1 Have your child stand on her preferred foot on the blue sticker with her knee bent. Support her back and rib cage as shown.

Helpful hints

- Be sure your child does the activity with help before she attempts it on her own.
- A span of time is usually needed in order to learn each step of the skill.
- If your child is left-foot dominant, reverse right and left sides when following the instructions.
- Ask your child to focus forward throughout the activity.
- You may find "Jump on one foot" to be a helpful instruction in teaching this skill, since your child already knows what jumping is and may not understand the command to hop.
- Give your child a gentle boost if needed, but do not lift her off the ground.
- Remember: the blue axis runs head to toe, the yellow axis runs front to back, and the red axis runs side to side.

Let's play

Play the Bunny Hop with your child. Hold her hands and practice hopping in different directions. Have your child hop forward as you hop backward, and vice versa. Have your child hop to the left as you hop to the right so you hop sideways together, then switch directions. Have your child hop to one side while you hop to the other. You can also play a new game of Bunny Rabbit Says.

2 Say "Hop up and down" as you help her take off on one foot and land in place on the same foot.

Repeat the activity, standing in front of your child and holding her hands at chest level. Hop up and down together.

(continued)

THE BUNNY HOP *(continued)*

3 Return to the starting position. Say "Hop yellow" as you help her take off on one foot and land on the same foot on the yellow sticker 8 inches forward.

Repeat, standing in front of your child and holding her hands at chest level. Have her hop forward as you hop backward.

Repeat the activity with your child hopping backward. When your child can do this well, go on to step 4.

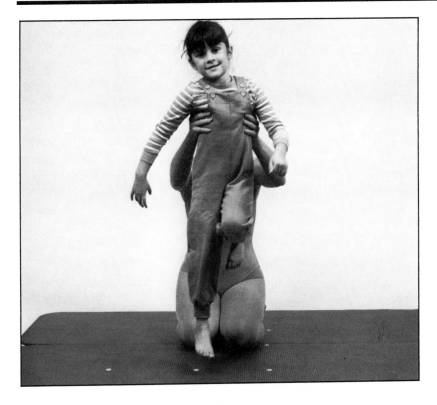

4 Assume the starting position again. Say "Hop red" as you help her take off on one foot and land on the same foot on the red sticker 8 inches to the side.

Repeat, standing in front of your child and holding her hands at chest level. Hop sideways together.

Repeat the activity, hopping to the other side.

STEPS TO SKILL MASTERY

1. Child hops in place once.
2. Child hops in place three times in a row.
   Age learned _____   **Average age learned:** 48 months
3. Child hops forward and backward once.
4. Child hops forward and backward three times in a row.
   Age learned _____   **Average age learned:** 48 months
5. Child hops sideways once.
6. Child hops sideways three times in a row.
   Age learned _____   **Average age learned:** 60 months

78 THE ONE-FOOT POINTER

GOAL 1: Your child balances on her preferred foot for 5 seconds.

GOAL 2: Your child balances on her right foot with her left leg extended backward and toes pointed for 5 seconds.

GOAL 3: Your child balances on her left foot with her right leg extended backward and toes pointed for 5 seconds.

REQUIRED SKILL: Your child can balance on either foot independently for 2 seconds (**49**).

Soon your child will be playing Hopscotch and learning to kick a ball. The One-Foot Pointer helps your child master the balancing skills needed for these games and strengthens thigh and calf muscles. When first attempting this exercise, allow your child to lean forward slightly to compensate for the weight of her extended free leg. Gradually she will learn to extend her arms to keep her own balance.

Before you begin
• Be sure your child is barefoot.
• Clear a flat, matted surface and place a colored

1 Have your child stand with her feet shoulder width apart, and hold her hand out to her side at chest level, as shown. Tell her to stand on her preferred foot and raise the other foot slightly off the floor. Ask her to hold her balance for 5 seconds.

2 Repeat the activity, gradually releasing your grip so your child attempts to balance on her preferred foot independently. Have her place her fingertips on her shoulders to maintain better balance.
When your child can do this well, go on to step 3.

sticker on it. If possible, set up a floor-length mirror nearby.
• Demonstrate the skill slowly.

Helpful hints
• Be sure your child does the activity with help before she attempts it on her own.
• A span of time is usually needed in order to learn each step of the skill.
• Ask your child to focus forward, and say "Stand on one leg" as you encourage her to balance.
• Never hold her hands at shoulder level or above, or you will disturb her center of balance.

Let's play
The object of this game is to have your child extend her leg and point out something with it, without using hands or words. Ask your child to close her eyes, then take a favorite toy and place it on the floor 2 or 3 feet away in any direction. Then ask "Where is your toy?" The child opens her eyes and points at the toy with her leg. You can also use objects in the room, saying "Where is the window? Where is the table? Where is Mommy?" and so forth. Repeat the game using the other leg.

3 Have your child extend her arms to the side at chest level and balance on her right leg. Place one hand around her stomach as shown and, with your free hand on her left shin, gently extend her leg behind her. Ask her to point her toes and hold the position for 5 seconds.
Repeat, having your child balance on her left foot and point her right foot straight behind her.

(continued)

THE ONE-FOOT POINTER (continued)

4 Ask your child to balance on her preferred foot with her free leg extended forward. If she needs assistance, place your hand under her calf.

Repeat, extending the other leg forward.

5 Ask your child to balance on her preferred foot with her free leg extended sideward. Place your hand under her calf if she needs help.

Repeat, extending the other leg sideward.

STEPS TO SKILL MASTERY

1. Child balances on her preferred foot independently for 5 seconds.
   Age learned _____ **Average age learned:** 48 months
2. Child balances on her right leg with her left foot pointed backward for 5 seconds.
   Age learned _____ **Average age learned:** 54 months
3. Child balances on her left leg with her right foot pointed backward for 5 seconds.
   Age learned _____ **Average age learned:** 54 months
4. Child balances on one leg with her free foot pointed forward for 5 seconds.
5. Child balances on one leg with her free foot pointed sideways for 5 seconds.

79 **TARGET TIME**

GOAL: Your child throws a ball overhand through a target 10 feet away.

REQUIRED SKILL: Your child can throw a ball underhand for 6 feet (**67**).

Earlier throwing activities stressed the movement and control of the arm rather than aim. At this level of development, children are ready to take on greater challenges. Target Time gives your child a sense of mastery as she learns to throw with accuracy.

Before you begin
• Clear a flat, matted surface near an open doorway.
• Have available a 5-inch foam or plastic ball.
• Demonstrate slowly throwing overhand through the doorway.

1 Have your child stand 10 feet in front of an open doorway with her arms down at her sides. Standing behind her, grasp the back of her preferred hand and lift it straight up overhead and back.

2 Say "Throw" as you swing your child's hand forward. Release your grip and ask her to swing her arm back and forth several times until she can do it consistently by herself.

Helpful hints

• Be sure your child does the activity with help before she attempts it on her own.

• See that your child's arm points straight down, then overhead and back about 70 degrees to begin the throw (step 1), and forward to the same angle at the end (step 2).

• Encourage your child to focus on the target at all times.

• Be sure she does *not* release the ball until her hand is forward about 70 degrees.

• Your child should swing her arm back and forth in a straight line. It should not cross in front of her body.

STEPS TO SKILL MASTERY

1. Child throws a ball overhand through a target 10 feet away.

   Age learned _____   **Average age learned:** 48 months

2. Child throws a ball overhand through a target three times in a row.

3 Give your child the ball and ask her to throw it through the doorway using the arm motion in step 2. Repeat three times.

80 KICKBALL

GOAL: Your child kicks a large ball to a target 10 feet away.

REQUIRED SKILLS: Your child can balance on one foot (**52**), and can catch a bounced ball (**70-1**).

Children enjoy kicking activities because they feel a sense of their own power when they see the effect a good kick can have on a ball. For an uncoordinated child, however, no sport or game is much fun to play. Kids tend to lack proficiency in kicking because foot-eye coordination develops later than hand-eye skills. Kickball promotes accurate foot-eye control, which is vital to many play activities.

Before you begin
• Clear a flat surface.

1 Have your child stand on one foot 10 feet away from the target. Be sure her preferred leg is lifted off the ground, her knee is bent and her foot is pointing behind her.

2 Encourage your child to focus on the target. Then have her extend her bent leg straight forward as you say "Kick." Repeat until the swinging motion is consistent.

• Have available a 9- or 11-inch plastic or rubber ball and a chair or other target.
• Demonstrate kicking at the target slowly.

Helpful hints

• Be sure your child's leg points back about 70 degrees to begin the kick (step 1), and forward to the same angle at the end (step 2).
• If necessary, hold your child's bent leg just below the knee and gently extend it forward to assist. Be sure it does *not* swing to the side.

3 Repeat step 1, placing the ball on the ground just in front of your child's lifted foot. Then have your child repeat the leg-swinging motion in step 2 to kick the ball forward. Be sure she focuses on the target and swings her foot straight through. Repeat three times.

Repeat, aiming to kick the ball to the target.

81 **THE PUTTER**

GOAL: Your child strikes a ball placed on the floor with a plastic mallet.

REQUIRED SKILL: Your child can catch a bounced ball (**70-1**).

The putter is a ground-level arm stroke such as that used in golf or hockey. Your child will enjoy testing her power and aim, so watch out for UFOs as she learns this new way to send things in motion.

Before you begin
• Clear a flat surface near an open doorway.
• Have available a 5-inch foam ball and a plastic mallet or bat.
• Demonstrate the activity slowly.

1 Stand behind your child and place the mallet in her hands so that her preferred hand is above her other hand when the mallet is held upright. Keep your hands on hers and pull the mallet sideward about 70 degrees.

2 Say "Strike" as you swing the mallet back down toward the floor, then up and through to 70 degrees in the opposite direction. Release your grip and ask your child to swing the mallet several times by herself between the starting and follow-through positions until the motion is consistent.

Helpful hint

• Be sure your child does the activity with help before she attempts it on her own.

STEPS TO SKILL MASTERY

1. Child strikes a foam ball on the floor with a mallet.
   Age learned _____   **Average age learned:** 48 months
2. Child strikes a ball on the floor through a doorway 6 feet away.

3 Place the ball about 4 inches in front of your child's feet. Ask her to focus on the ball, then hold the mallet in the starting position and use the same swing to strike it. If necessary, hold her forearms lightly to assist.

Repeat, having your child strike the ball through a doorway 6 feet away.

82 BRIDGES AND MONKEYS

GOAL 1: Your child hangs on a bar above her reach in a pike position.

GOAL 2: Your child hangs on a bar above her reach and swings back and forth three times in a row.

REQUIRED SKILLS: Your child can demonstrate the basic body positions (**48**) and can hang on a bar in a tuck position for 5 seconds (**72**).

Bridges and Monkeys is a tough test of your child's arm and stomach strength. Holding the legs at a right angle to the body in a pike position while hanging from a bar requires more muscle power than any previous skill. Swinging on the bar combines strength with rhythm, which is important for developing good coordination. The achievement of these goals will help build your child's self-confidence.

Before you begin

• Securely hang a sturdy rod 1 inch in diameter in a doorway at a height 6 inches above your child's reach, or use a jungle gym crossbar at a playground.

1 Have your child stand with the bar 6 inches in front of her. Ask her to look at the bar and reach her arms toward it. Say "Hold on" as you gently lift her up to the bar in a straight-hang position as shown. Say "Pike" as you release your grip, and encourage her to hang with her legs at a right angle to her body and hold it for 5 seconds. Assist her off the bar.

Repeat the activity, telling your child to hang in the pike position for 10 seconds.

Be sure there is a soft, flat surface under the bar. Do not try this activity on a concrete playground.
• Demonstrate the activity slowly. Use a doll if you do not have a bar 6 inches above your own height.

Helpful hints

• Be sure your child does the activity with help before she attempts it on her own.
• Be sure your child uses a tight overhand grip on the bar. Her arms should hang straight.
• If necessary, hold your child's forearm with one hand and gently lift up her legs from the back of her lower thighs to assist.

Let's play

Have your child hang on the bar in a straight position. Tell her to lift her legs straight up like a drawbridge, "to let the boats go through." Pass toy boats or other large toys under the bridge. Have her slowly lower her legs after the boats have gone through. To develop swinging, play Monkeys with your child. Pretend the room is a jungle and she is a monkey swinging on the branches as she hangs from the bar. Make jungle noises and monkey sounds for fun. Be sure to maintain your spotting position at all times.

2 Ask your child to assume the pike position as before. Say "Swing" and ask her to quickly lower her legs and kick her heels behind her. Repeat three times. Assist her off the bar.

Repeat step 2, having your child swing five times in a row.

STEPS TO SKILL MASTERY

1. Child hangs with her legs in a pike for 5 seconds.
   Age learned _____ **Average age learned:** 48 months
2. Child hangs with her legs in a pike for 10 seconds.
3. Child swings back and forth three times independently.
   Age learned _____ **Average age learned:** 48 months
4. Child swings back and forth five times.

83 LEAPING UP AND OVER

GOAL 1: Your child leaps forward.
GOAL 2: Your child leaps sideways.

REQUIRED SKILL: Your child can hop on one foot (**77**).

In a leap, your child pushes off on one foot and lands on the other. It is a handy skill to have when a child plays near puddles, anthills, flower beds, sleeping kittens or any other small obstacles that might be lying in her path. The leap requires your youngster to keep track of her movement by using her muscle sense as she learns to coordinate her legs in flight.

Before you begin
• Be sure your child is barefoot.
• Clear a flat, matted surface. Place two yellow stickers 8 inches apart and 8 inches ahead of the starting

1 Have your child stand on her left leg at the starting position. Support her back and rib cage with your hands. Ask her to focus forward on the toy and bend her left knee.

2 Say "Leap yellow" as you help her take off on the left foot and land 8 inches ahead on the opposite foot.

Repeat, standing beside your child and holding her hand at chest level. Leap forward together.

Repeat the activity, this time beginning on the right leg.

position on the mat. Place a toy about 5 feet in front of your child.
• Demonstrate the activity slowly.

Helpful hints
• Be sure your child does the activity with help before she attempts it on her own.
• If your child is left-foot dominant, reverse right and left sides when following the instructions.
• If your child needs assistance, lift her up and tell her to swing her leading foot in the direction she is moving.

Let's play
Place several small objects, such as magazines, toys or cut-out shapes, on the floor and ask your child to pretend they are puddles she must leap over without getting her feet wet.

STEPS TO SKILL MASTERY
1. Child leaps forward from her left to her right foot.
   Age learned _____ **Average age learned:** 48 months
2. Child leaps forward from her right to her left foot.
3. Child leaps sideways from her left to her right foot.
   Age learned _____ **Average age learned:** 48 months
4. Child leaps sideways from her right to her left foot.

3 Assume the starting position again. Say "Leap red" as you help your child take off on her left foot and land 8 inches to the right on the opposite foot.

Repeat, standing beside your child and holding her hand at chest level. Leap sideways together.

Repeat the activity, using the right leg to start, leaping to the left side.

84 TRAVELING MONKEYS

GOAL: Your child hangs on a bar above her reach and takes four hand steps to the right.

REQUIRED SKILL: Your child can swing on a bar (**82-2**).

Traveling Monkeys combines a test of power and coordination. To move along the bar, a child must learn to hold the weight of her body with one arm as she controls her motion with the other. Once she discovers how to use her arms and hands as a mode of locomotion, your child will want to try out her skills on every jungle gym and tree.

Before you begin
• Securely hang a sturdy rod 1 inch in diameter in a doorway at a height 6 inches above your child's

1 Have your child stand with the bar 6 inches in front of her reach. Ask her to look at the bar and reach her arms toward it. Say "Hold on" as you gently lift her up to the bar in a straight-hang position, as shown.

reach, or use a jungle gym crossbar at a playground. Be sure there is a soft, flat surface under the bar.
• Demonstrate the activity slowly. Use a doll if you do not have a bar 6 inches above your own height.

Helpful hints

• Be sure your child does the activity with help before she attempts it on her own.
• Be sure your child uses a tight overhand grip on the bar. Her arms should hang straight.

Let's play

Have your child hang in a straight position on one end of the bar and pretend she is a monkey in a tree. Ask her to try to walk her hands across the branch four times, like a traveling monkey, to get to the other side of an imaginary swamp.

STEPS TO SKILL MASTERY

1. Child takes four hand steps to the right.
   Age learned _____ **Average age learned:** 54 months
2. Child takes four hand steps to the left.

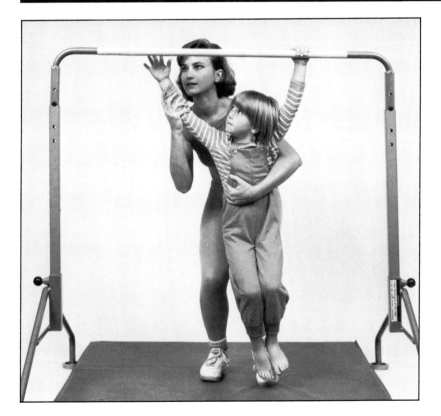

2 Stand behind your child and wrap your left arm around the front of her torso. Place your right hand over hers and gently slide it a few inches to the right as you say "Walk your hands" or "Hand step." Then move her left hand toward her right hand. Gradually release your grip and encourage her to hand step on her own in the same direction.
Repeat the activity, encouraging your child to hand step toward the left.

Before you continue, turn back to the goals listed below. These skills should be learned before you introduce the next exercise.
64/Squash the Bugs, Goal 3   **78/The One-Foot Pointer, Goal 3**
78/The One-Foot Pointer, Goal 2

85 HOPSCOTCH HOP

GOAL 1: Your child jumps forward from two feet to one foot.
GOAL 2: Your child jumps sideways from two feet to one foot.

REQUIRED SKILL: Your child can hop from one foot to two feet (**64-2**).

As your child begins to participate in more sophisticated games and sports, she will discover that she can accomplish many difficult motor activities simply by combining familiar skills in novel ways. Hopscotch Hop draws on your child's body control, coordination and balancing skills to attain a higher level of mastery. Jumping from two feet to one foot, a skill exercised in the popular children's game of Hopscotch, is known as *sissone.*

Before you begin

• Be sure your child is barefoot.
• Clear a flat, matted surface. On the mat, mark two starting positions with *X*'s 4 inches apart. Center a yellow sticker 8 inches in front of the two starting positions, and place a red sticker 8 inches to the left of the left-hand starting marker.
• Demonstrate the activity slowly.

1 Have your child stand on the starting stickers with feet shoulder width apart and knees bent. Support her back and rib cage as shown.

2 Say "Jump from two to one on yellow" as you assist her in landing on one foot on the yellow sticker in front of her.

Repeat, standing beside your child and holding her hands at chest level. Do the sissone forward together.

Do the activity again but land on the other foot.

When your child can do this well, go on to step 3.

Helpful hints

• Be sure your child does the activity with help before she attempts it on her own.

• A span of time is usually needed in order to learn each step of the skill.

• If your child is left-foot dominant, reverse right and left sides when following the instructions.

• Ask your child to focus forward on the yellow sticker throughout the activity.

• If necessary, lift her up slightly and say "One foot down" to assist.

• Never pull your child's arms or hold them above chest level, or you will disturb her center of balance.

<table>
<tr><td colspan="2">STEPS TO SKILL MASTERY</td></tr>
</table>

STEPS TO SKILL MASTERY

1. Child jumps forward from two feet to one foot.
   Age learned _____   **Average age learned:** 54 months
2. Child jumps forward from two feet to one foot three times in a row.
3. Child jumps sideways from two feet to one foot.
   Age learned _____   **Average age learned:** 60 months
4. Child jumps sideways from two feet to one foot three times in a row.

3 Assume the starting position again. Say "Jump from two to one on red" as you assist her in landing on one foot on the red sticker to the left. Be sure your child lands on her outside foot.

Repeat, standing beside your child and holding her hands at chest level. Do the sissone *sideways together.*

Do the activity again, jumping to the other side.

Before you continue, turn back to the goal listed below. This skill should be learned before you introduce the next exercise.
77/The Bunny Hop, Goal 3

86 SHAPES AND CIRCLES

Shapes and Circles develops the fine motor control necessary for later writing skills. Drawing geometric shapes also improves the understanding of spatial concepts fundamental to cognitive development.

GOAL: Your child draws basic shapes.

REQUIRED SKILL: Your child can draw a horizontal and vertical line (**62**).

Before you begin
• Be sure the room is well lit.
• Set up a chair and table suited to your child's height.
• Have available a pencil or crayon and drawing paper.
• Demonstrate the skill slowly.

1 On a sheet of paper, draw four dots 6 inches apart, to mark the corners of a square. Put the paper down in front of your seated child, and place the pencil or crayon in her preferred hand, positioning her thumb, forefinger and middle finger as shown. With your hands over hers, place the pencil point on the upper-left-hand dot on the paper. Say "Draw" as you move her hand to the right, down, to the left and up to connect the dots. Draw four more dots and repeat.

Helpful hint

• Ask your child to focus on the pencil or crayon point as she draws.

STEPS TO SKILL MASTERY

1. Child draws 6-inch basic shapes by connecting dots.
   Age learned _____ **Average age learned:** 60 months
2. Child draws 6-inch basic shapes without dots.

2 Repeat the activity, holding your child's forearm. Gradually release your grip to enable your child to try the skill on her own.

Repeat the activity, drawing a triangle, a rectangle and a circle.

87 THE BODY BUILDER

GOAL: Your child holds her chin up on a bar in a flexed-arm hang for 2 seconds.

REQUIRED SKILL: Your child can hand step across a bar (**84**).

To do The Body Builder, a child must have the muscle power to hold the entire weight of her body by her arms. This strength is important for the safety and self-confidence of the active child as she tests her motor abilities in the playground or on the monkey bars.

Before you begin
• Securely hang a sturdy bar 1 inch in diameter in a doorway at a height 6 inches above your child's reach, or use a jungle gym crossbar at a playground.

1 Have your child stand with the bar 6 inches in front of her reach. Ask her to look at the bar and reach her arms toward it. Say "Hang on" as you gently lift her up to the bar in a hang position.

Be sure there is a soft, flat surface under the bar.
• Demonstrate the activity slowly. Use a doll if you do not have a bar 6 inches above your own height.

Helpful hints

• Be sure your child does the activity with help before she attempts it on her own.
• Be sure your child uses a tight overhand grip on the bar. To start, her arms should hang straight.
• Do not let her rest her chin on the bar.

STEPS TO SKILL MASTERY

1. Child holds the flexed-arm hang for 2 seconds.
   Age learned _____   **Average age learned:** 60 months
2. Child holds the flexed-arm hang for 5 seconds.

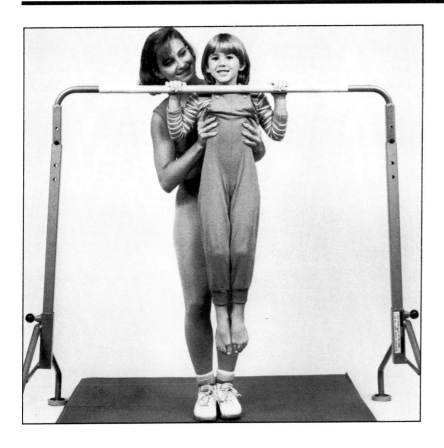

2 Ask your child to pull her chin up to the bar. Say "Chin up" or "Pull up" as you help lift her to a flexed-arm hang, holding her back and rib cage. Have her hold for 2 seconds, then assist her off the bar.

Repeat, gradually providing less help so your child attempts to pull her chin to the bar on her own power.

Repeat until your child holds the flexed-arm hang for 5 seconds.

88 WALKING THE PLANK

GOAL: Your child walks backward along a floor beam independently.

REQUIRED SKILL: Your child can walk sideways and forward along a floor beam independently (**62**).

Walking the Plank challenges your child to move her body without looking where she is going, so she has to feel her success without seeing it. The ability to control a movement by the way it feels rather than by visual reference is essential to higher-level skills.

Before you begin
• Place a 4-inch-wide, 8-foot-long floor beam on a flat, matted surface.
• Have a toy available.

1 Have your child stand at one end of the beam with her feet shoulder width apart and parallel, and her arms extended to the side at chest level. Holding her hand lightly, have her make a quarter turn so she ends up standing with her right foot slightly behind her left, as shown.

2 Say "Step slowly" as you help her step backward on her right foot. Ask her to place her left foot behind her right, then her right foot behind her left along the length of the beam. Assist her off.

Repeat the activity, gradually releasing your grip until your child walks backward along the beam independently.

- Be sure your child is barefoot.
- Demonstrate the activity slowly.

Helpful hints
- Be sure your child does the activity with help before she attempts it on her own.
- Ask your child to focus forward on a toy placed 4 feet away and not on her feet.
- If she falls off the beam, have her get back on at the point where she fell and continue to the end.

Let's play
This is the age when children love to pretend. Ask your child to imagine she is the captain of a ship captured by pirates. Have her mount the beam and slowly walk along it backward, as if she were walking the plank of a pirate ship. Pretend you are an evil pirate, and describe the alligators and other dangers in the waters below as you encourage her to get to the other side. Assist her as necessary. When she makes it to the end, she becomes the pirate and you have to walk the plank!

3 Repeat the activity, having your child walk backward along the beam on tiptoe.

STEPS TO SKILL MASTERY
1. Child walks backward along the floor beam independently.
   Age learned _____   **Average age learned:** 60 months
2. Child walks backward along the floor beam on tiptoe.

89 **THE BATTER**

GOAL: Your child strikes a ball at waist level with a plastic bat.

REQUIRED SKILL: Your child can strike a ball on the floor through a doorway 6 feet away (**81**).

Practicing striking skills develops a child's ability to control the force and direction of her own movement at the same time she controls the motion and force of the tool in her hand. The Batter is a mid-height arm stroke such as that used in baseball or racket sports.

Before you begin
• Clear a flat surface near an open doorway.
• Have available a 5-inch foam ball, a batting tee

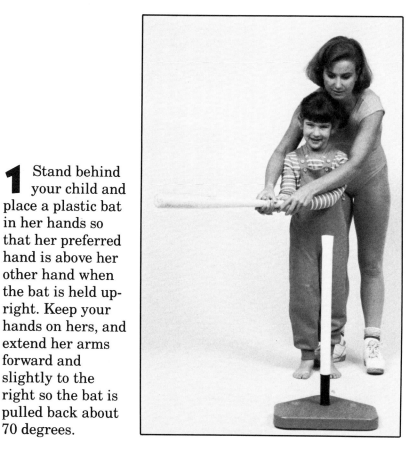

1 Stand behind your child and place a plastic bat in her hands so that her preferred hand is above her other hand when the bat is held upright. Keep your hands on hers, and extend her arms forward and slightly to the right so the bat is pulled back about 70 degrees.

2 Say "Strike" as you swing the bat forward and slightly beyond the corresponding angle on the opposite side of her body. Release your grip and ask your child to swing the bat several times by herself between the two positions until the motion is consistent.

and a plastic bat. If you don't have a batting tee, attach the ball to a string and hang it at your child's waist level.

• Demonstrate the activity slowly.

Helpful hint

• In midheight striking skills, the ball moves straight sideways when hit correctly, so be sure your child is facing perpendicular to the doorway. Make sure the middle of the bat strikes the ball when your child's arms are extended forward.

STEPS TO SKILL MASTERY

1. Child strikes a foam ball placed at waist level with a bat.
   Age learned _____   **Average age learned:** 60 months
2. Child strikes a ball placed at waist level through a doorway 6 feet away.

3 Place the ball on the batting tee at your child's waist level directly in front of her. Ask her to focus on the ball, then hold the bat in the starting position and use exactly the same swing to strike it. If necessary, hold her forearms lightly to assist.

Repeat, having your child strike the ball through a doorway 6 feet away.

90 **BRIDGE UP!**♦

GOAL: Your child holds a back bend ("bridge") for 5 seconds.

REQUIRED SKILL: Your child can do five modified push-ups (**71**).

Bridge Up! develops greater arm, back and leg strength. This skill also expands a child's spatial awareness as she learns to control the movement of her body while upside down. Experiencing the world from this point of view gives a child a greater sense of freedom.

Before you begin
• Clear a flat, matted surface.
• Demonstrate the activity slowly. Use a doll if you cannot perform the skill.

1 Have your child lie on her back on the mat and bend her knees so that her feet are flat on the floor close to her body. Then have her lift both arms over her head and place her hands under her shoulders, with her palms on the mat and her fingertips pointing toward her feet. Stand straddling your child with your feet near her hips and grasp her back and rib cage.

Helpful hint
• Be sure your child does the activity with help before she attempts it on her own.

Let's play
Learning the Bridge Up! skill is more fun when you add a little imagination. Follow the coaching instructions, but ask your child to pretend she is a drawbridge over a river. Make believe a toy boat or duck is sailing toward the bridge. As you move the toy toward your child on the mat, give the command to "Bridge up" to let the boat sail under.

STEPS TO SKILL MASTERY

1. Child holds a back bend for 5 seconds.
   Age learned _____   **Average age learned:** 60 months
2. Child does three back bends in a row.

2 Say "Bridge up" as you gently lift your child into a back bend. Ask her to look back at her hands and hold the bridge position for 5 seconds. Lower her back to the mat.

Repeat three times in a row, gradually providing less assistance to allow your child to bridge up on her own.

91 **TOPS AND CLOCKS**

GOAL 1: Your child spins completely around on one foot.
GOAL 2: Your child jumps up and turns in a complete circle.

REQUIRED SKILL: Your child can hop on one foot three times in a row (**77-2**).

Spinning and turning are exhilarating experiences for most youngsters. Once they get the knack, they will fling themselves around with great abandon and glee. In addition to being fun, Tops and Clocks teaches rotation skills, developing your child's balance and control, and shows children that they have a "sidedness" as they experience for themselves that jumping and turning in one direction is much easier than doing it in the other.

Before you begin
• Be sure your child is barefoot.
• Clear a flat, matted surface. Tape a starting-position sticker in the center of the mat. Place another four stickers or toys 4 feet to the left, right,

1 To start, have your child stand on the ball of her right foot on the starting sticker with her arms extended to the left. Ask her to focus forward on the north marker.

front and back of the starting position, like the four directions on a compass.
• Demonstrate the activity slowly.

Helpful hints
• Remember: the blue axis runs head to toe.
• Remind your child to keep her body blue—that is, upright on the blue axis—when she jumps and turns. There is a tendency for children to get red in their blue when jumping—that is, to bend their upper torso forward on the red axis.
• If your child is left-foot dominant, reverse right and left sides when following the instructions.
• Ask your child to lift her right heel off the ground if she doesn't understand the instruction to stand on the ball of her foot.

Let's play
To practice spinning on one foot, have your child pretend she is a top. Have her pretend to be the hands on a clock. Call out an hour and your child can practice jumping up and turning to the proper position on the clock.

2 Say "Spin" and ask your child to swing her arms to the right and pivot on her right foot until she is facing south. Ask her to spin another half turn back to north.
Repeat, having your child spin completely around.
Repeat steps 1 and 2, having your child spin on her other leg.

(continued)

TOPS AND CLOCKS *(continued)*

3 To start, have your child stand with her feet shoulder width apart and tell her to focus forward on the north marker. Say "Jump and turn" and ask her to jump a quarter turn to east.

Repeat until she can do this well.

4 From the starting position, ask her to jump a half turn to south.

Repeat until she can do this well.

STEPS TO SKILL MASTERY

1. Child spins completely around on her preferred foot.
   Age learned _____   **Average age learned:** 60 months
2. Child spins completely around on her other foot.
3. Child jumps up and turns completely around in one direction.
   Age learned _____   **Average age learned:** 60 months
4. Child jumps up and turns completely around in both directions.

5 From the starting position, ask her to jump a full turn back to north.

Repeat steps 3 through 5, having your child jump and turn to her other side.

92 THE DONKEY KICK

GOAL: Your child supports her body weight in a handstand.

REQUIRED SKILLS: Your child can hang in a tuck (**72**) and can hold a back bend for 5 seconds (**90**).

While most kids can hop, skip and jump, not every kid on the block can do a handstand. Your child's self-confidence will get a big boost when she learns this complex skill. By being able to control her body when upside down as well as upright, she'll also be better equipped than most kids at the playground to recover her balance safely if she loses it.

Before you begin
• Clear a flat, matted surface. Place five stickers on it as shown:
(If your child is left-handed, place the left-foot sticker at 18 inches and the right-foot sticker at 24

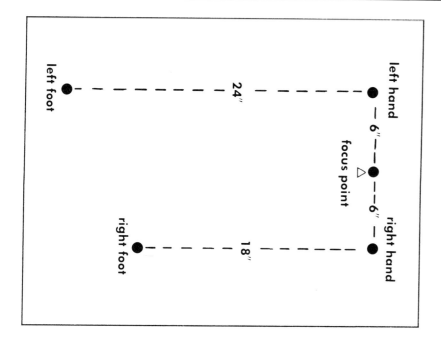

1 Have your child place her hands and feet on the stickers, and ask her to focus on the sticker between her hands. Kneel to her left side, placing your left hand under her chest and your right hand under her left leg, just below the knee.

inches. Adjust the placement of the stickers according to your child's height.)

• Demonstrate kicking up to a handstand slowly. Use a doll if you cannot perform the skill.

Helpful hints

• Be sure your child does the activity with help before she attempts it on her own.

• Be sure your child keeps focusing on the sticker and does *not* bend her arms or place her head on the floor.

Let's play

For added fun, ask your child to kick her feet up in the air and bray like a donkey while practicing the activity.

STEPS TO SKILL MASTERY

1. Child supports her body weight in the handstand position.
   Age learned _____ **Average age learned:** 72 months
2. Child kicks up to a handstand three times in a row.

2 Say "Kick up" as you gently lift her legs off the ground while supporting her chest. Assist her in lowering her legs back to the mat.

Repeat the activity, gradually providing less assistance so your child attempts to kick up to a handstand independently.

93 **THE LOBBER**

GOAL: Your child strikes a ball placed above her reach with a plastic bat.

REQUIRED SKILL: Your child can strike a ball placed at waist level through a doorway 6 feet away (**89**).

Life in the schoolyard or playground is tough on the kids who don't fit in because they aren't as physically skillful as their peers. Children who have good striking skills are able to pick up new games more easily and join in activities successfully. The Lobber is a high arm stroke such as that used in a tennis serve.

Before you begin
• Have available a 5-inch foam or plastic ball and a plastic bat.
• Demonstrate the activity slowly and with effort.

1 Stand behind your child and place a plastic bat in her hands with her preferred hand above her other. Keep your hands on hers and lift her arms so the bat is pulled back about 70 degrees and slightly over her shoulder.

2 Say "Strike" as you swing the bat directly forward to the corresponding angle on the opposite side of her body. Release your grip and ask your child to swing the bat several times by herself between the two positions until the motion is consistent.

Helpful hint
• Make sure the middle of the bat makes contact with the ball when your child's arms are extended forward.

STEPS TO SKILL MASTERY

1. Child strikes a ball placed 12 inches above her reach with a bat.
   Age learned _____   **Average age learned:** 72 months
2. Child strikes a ball placed 12 inches above her reach three times in a row.

3 Hang a 5-inch foam or plastic ball on a string 12 inches above your child's reach. Stand your child directly under the ball and ask her to focus on it. Tell her to hold the bat in the starting position and use the same swing to strike it. Hold your child's forearms lightly if she needs help.

Repeat, having your child strike the ball three times in a row.

94 **GALLOPING HORSES**

GOAL: Your child gallops forward for 10 feet.

REQUIRED SKILLS: Your child can hop (**77**) and leap (**83**).

Galloping is a repeated, rapid stepping movement leading on the same forward foot. The rhythm of galloping is so familiar, you probably know how to mimic the sound by tapping on a table. Children develop an awareness of this rhythm as they ride their imaginary horses.

Before you begin
• Be sure your child is barefoot.
• Clear a flat, matted surface. Lay down a strip of tape 10 feet long.

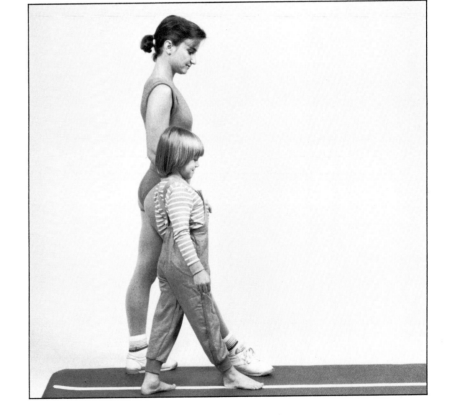

1 Have your child stand at one end of the tape with her feet shoulder width apart, focusing on the toy. Stand beside her and hold her hand. Ask your child to play follow the leader. Say "Gallop" as you step forward on your right foot.

- Place a toy at one end of the tape.
- Demonstrate the activity slowly.

Helpful hints
- If your child is left-foot dominant, reverse right and left feet when following the instructions.
- Be sure your child steps on the ball of her rear foot to create the familiar bounce of the gallop.

Let's play
Play Galloping Horses with your child. Ask her to gallop in a circle around the "corral," first slowly and then quickly. Then ask her to try it on her other foot, then backward.

STEPS TO SKILL MASTERY
1. Child gallops, leading with her preferred foot. **Age learned** _____ **Average age learned:** 72 months 2. Child gallops, leading with her other foot.

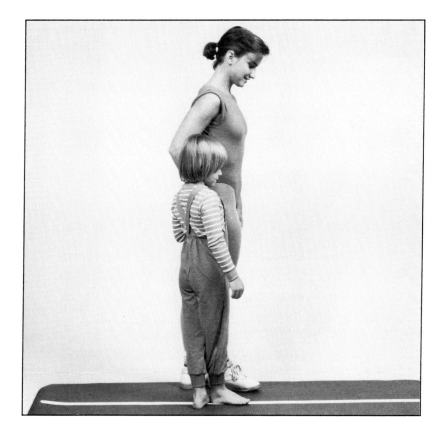

2 Close the left foot behind the right. Encourage your child to do the same, repeating this step-together motion slowly at first. Once your child picks up the step, speed up the pace of your movement until it resembles a gallop.
Repeat the activity, leading with the left foot.

95 SKIP TO MY LOU

GOAL: Your child skips forward for 10 feet.

REQUIRED SKILL: Your child can gallop (**94**).

The beat and bounce of a skip seem like natural expressions of joy, and it's true that children find skipping a delightful means of locomotion. The skip is a rhythmic, repeated step-hop movement leading on alternating feet. Unlike the gallop, which is a repeated step on one side of the body only, skipping requires the ability to transfer and repeat a complex step on the other side, too.

Before you begin
• Be sure your child is barefoot.
• Clear a flat, matted surface. Lay down a strip of tape 10 feet long.

1 Have your child stand at one end of the tape with her feet shoulder width apart, and tell her to focus on the toy. Stand beside her and hold her hand. Ask her to play follow the leader. Say "Skip" as you step forward on your right foot.

• Place a toy at one end of the tape.
• Demonstrate the activity slowly.

Helpful hint
• If your child is left-foot dominant, reverse right and left feet when following the instructions.

Let's play
Skip with your child as you sing "Skip to My Lou." Practice skipping around your house, to the store, to the playground or anywhere you happen to be going.

STEPS TO SKILL MASTERY

1. Child skips forward 10 feet.
   Age learned _____   **Average age learned:** 72 months
2. Child skips backward 10 feet.

2 Hop on your right foot, then repeat the movement, stepping forward and hopping on your left foot. Encourage your child to do the same as you repeat this step-hop motion slowly at first. Once your child picks up the step, speed up the pace until it resembles a skip.
Repeat the activity, skipping backward.

96 THE CARTWHEEL

GOAL: Your child begins to perform a cartwheel.

REQUIRED SKILLS: Your child can kick up to a handstand three times in a row (**92**).

The Cartwheel is an impressive display of a child's overall motor abilities, and your child will enjoy the feeling of mastery that comes from performing it. This difficult body rotation requires excellent strength, balance and coordination, and your youngster will proudly show off her new trick, especially if she discovers that even Mom or Dad can't do it!

Before you begin
• Be sure your child is barefoot.
• Clear a flat, matted surface. Lay down two 4-foot-long strips of white tape 4 inches apart. Place stickers as shown in the diagram:

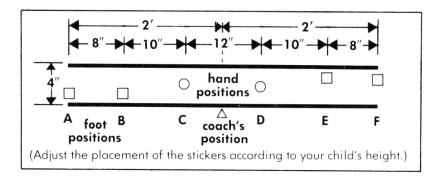

(Adjust the placement of the stickers according to your child's height.)

1 Have your child stand with her feet shoulder width apart, with her left foot on sticker *A* and her right foot on sticker *B*. Have her extend her right arm to the side and her left arm straight overhead. Kneel behind stickers *C* and *D* and, with your wrists crossed, grasp your child's back and sides, as shown.

2 Help your child rotate her body sideways to the right, so her right hand lands on *C* and her left on *D*. At the same time, she should begin to kick up her legs, lifting herself onto her hands.

• Demonstrate the cartwheel slowly, using a doll if you cannot do it yourself.

Helpful hints

• Be sure your child does the activity with help before she attempts it on her own.
• If your child is left-side dominant, reverse right and left sides when following the instructions.
• Say "Cartwheel kick," "Jump your feet up" or "Sideways donkey kick" when instructing your child. At first, her movement will look more like a donkey kicking its rear legs from side to side than a cartwheel. With time and practice, she will be able to straighten her legs and torso to perform a smooth rotation.
• Be sure she does not bend her arms or place her head on the ground.

STEPS TO SKILL MASTERY

1. Child begins to perform a cartwheel.
   Age learned _____ **Average age learned:** 72 months
2. Child performs a cartwheel independently.

---

3 Have your child look at stickers *E* and *F* as she moves her feet toward them.

4 Maintaining a secure grip at all times, help your child through the cartwheel kick as she lands with her left foot on *E* and her right on *F.*
Ask her to try the cartwheel on her own, keeping her legs straight.

8
KEEPING TRACK OF YOUR CHILD'S PROGRESS

If you would like a permanent record of your child's motor development, you will want to fill in the charts in this chapter, which track her progress in comparison to the "average growth curve."

The charts are an important means of measuring skill development. First of all, periodic evaluations let you modify your child's activities according to her progress in each skill area. For instance, if you see that she is physically strong for her age but slightly below average in learning fine motor skills, you might spend less time on strength-building activities but give her extra opportunities to do things with her hands and improve manual skills.

A caution about comparisons
The purpose of the Gerard Method is to foster well-rounded skill development. While all the skills in the program should be learned in progression by all children, this does not mean that all children will learn them as soon as the average or as well as the best. The average growth curve is shown on the graphs as a standard for comparison, but don't expect your youngster's progress to look exactly the same.

Understanding the charts
Each graph provides three points of reference: along the left column, it lists ages, in months; along the bottom, the numbered activities in their developmental (*not* numerical) sequence; and printed on the chart itself is a line showing the average pattern of skill learning.

In most cases, the "average age learned" was taken from scientific literature on the skill. Where no average age has been established by research, however, the age given is based on my personal experience teaching these activities to children.

This is all the information appearing on the charts —the rest you will fill in using your child's personal data.

Completing the charts
In the "Steps to Skill Mastery" section at the end of each activity, there is a place to record the age, in months, at which your child first learned the skill. This is the information you will plot on the graph.

First, locate the number of the skill on the bottom of the graph. Then move your pencil up the vertical bar until you reach the horizontal line corresponding to the age when your child learned the skill. Make a point on the graph where the two lines intersect. Draw a line connecting the points as you plot them. Your child's learning pattern may appear above or below the average one shown.

A note about the numbering

When an activity, such as The Straddle Hang (**58**), has a single objective, the number appears once on the bottom of the graph. However, some activities, such as Hang Loose, have multiple objectives: Goal 1, Goal 2 and so on. On the chart, these goals appear as **45-1** and **45-2** and are to be recorded separately.

The activity numbers do not always appear in order because of the time lapse in skill learning in multiple-goal activities. For example, look at the Level Two coordination chart on page 212. Catch a Balloon has two goals: **46-1** is learned an average of 12 months earlier than **46-2**, and in the interim other skills are learned, too.

If your child's growth is lagging

I recommend that at least once every three months you evaluate your child's development in relation to the average pattern of skill learning printed on each graph.

If your child's development appears to be lagging a few months behind the average—particularly during the first three years of life—bring it to the attention of your pediatrician immediately.

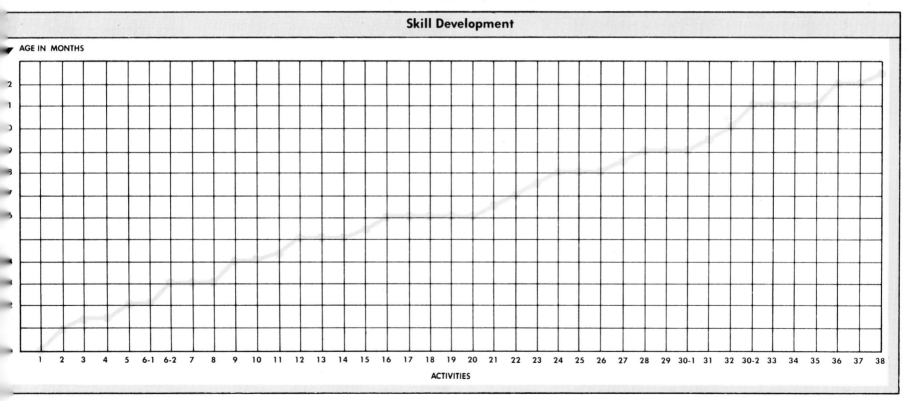

LEVEL ONE: BIRTH TO 12 MONTHS

Skill Development

AGE IN MONTHS

ACTIVITIES

LEVEL TWO: 1 TO 2½ YEARS

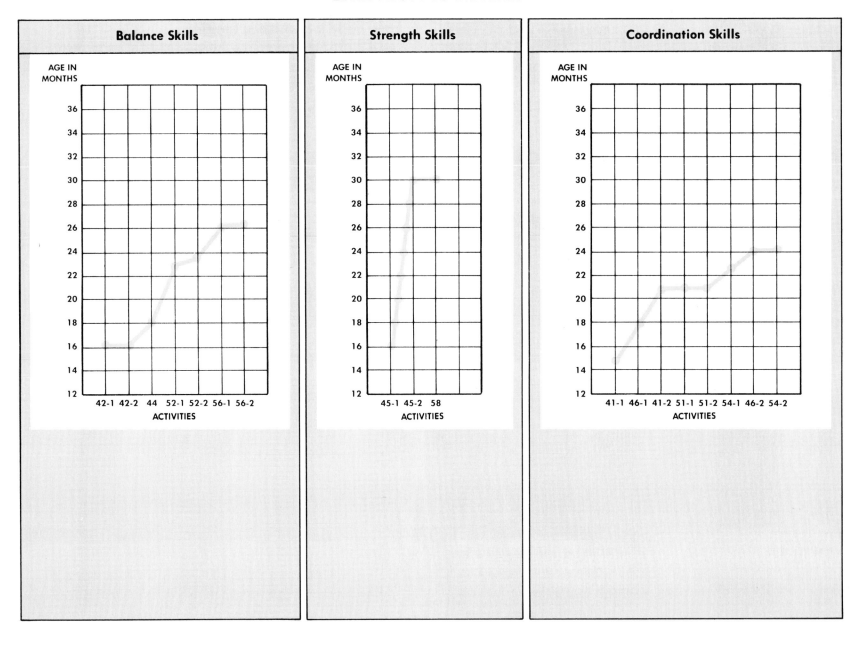

Balance Skills	Strength Skills	Coordination Skills

Balance Skills

AGE IN MONTHS

36, 34, 32, 30, 28, 26, 24, 22, 20, 18, 16, 14, 12

ACTIVITIES: 42-1 42-2 44 52-1 52-2 56-1 56-2

Strength Skills

AGE IN MONTHS

36, 34, 32, 30, 28, 26, 24, 22, 20, 18, 16, 14, 12

ACTIVITIES: 45-1 45-2 58

Coordination Skills

AGE IN MONTHS

36, 34, 32, 30, 28, 26, 24, 22, 20, 18, 16, 14, 12

ACTIVITIES: 41-1 46-1 41-2 51-1 51-2 54-1 46-2 54-2

LEVEL TWO: 1 TO 2½ YEARS

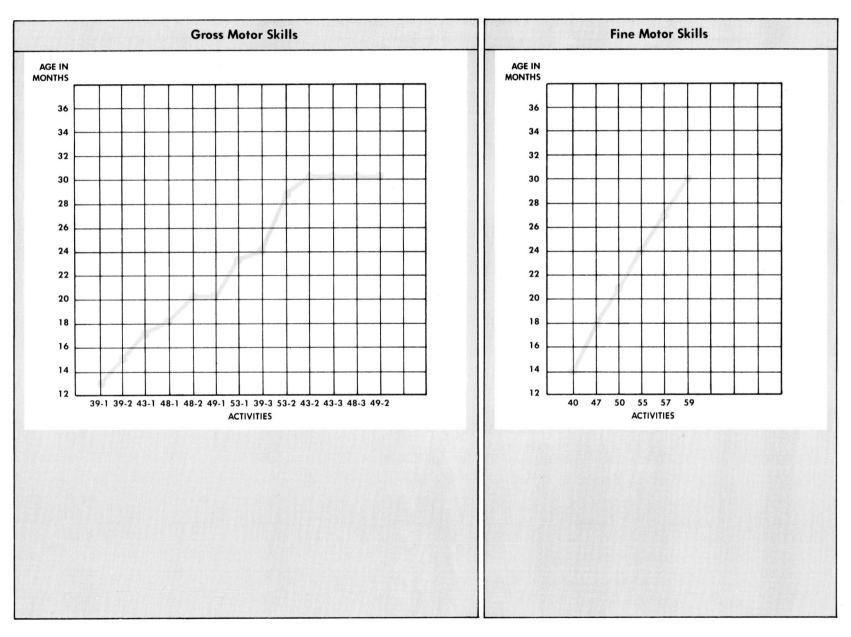

Gross Motor Skills

AGE IN
MONTHS

36
34
32
30
28
26
24
22
20
18
16
14
12

39-1 39-2 43-1 48-1 48-2 49-1 53-1 39-3 53-2 43-2 43-3 48-3 49-2
ACTIVITIES

Fine Motor Skills

AGE IN
MONTHS

36
34
32
30
28
26
24
22
20
18
16
14
12

40   47   50   55   57   59
ACTIVITIES

LEVEL THREE: 2½ TO 6 YEARS

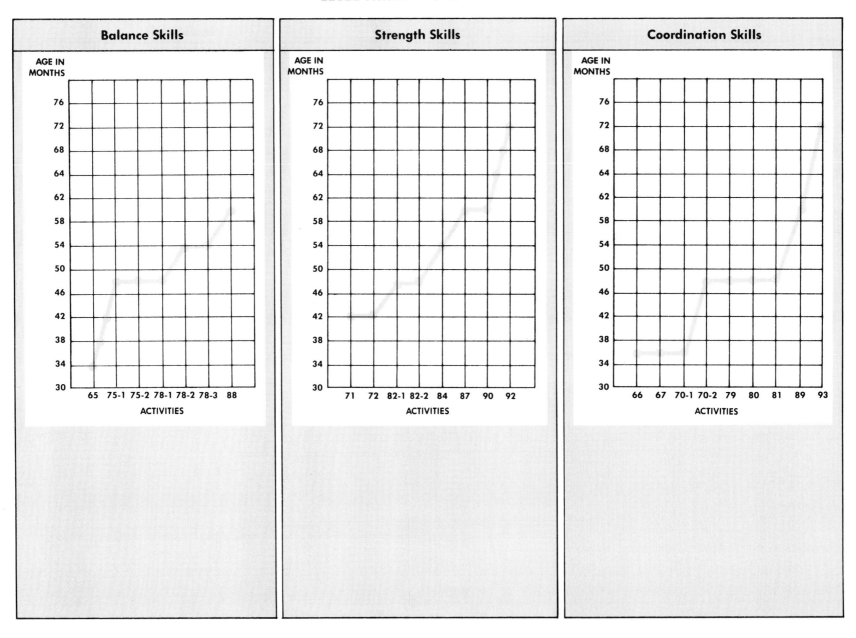

Balance Skills

AGE IN MONTHS

76
72
68
64
62
58
54
50
46
42
38
34
30

65 75-1 75-2 78-1 78-2 78-3 88
ACTIVITIES

Strength Skills

AGE IN MONTHS

76
72
68
64
62
58
54
50
46
42
38
34
30

71 72 82-1 82-2 84 87 90 92
ACTIVITIES

Coordination Skills

AGE IN MONTHS

76
72
68
64
62
58
54
50
46
42
38
34
30

66 67 70-1 70-2 79 80 81 89 93
ACTIVITIES

LEVEL THREE: 2½ TO 6 YEARS

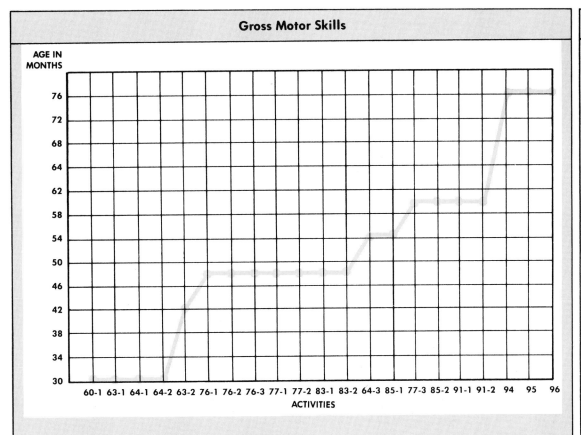

Gross Motor Skills

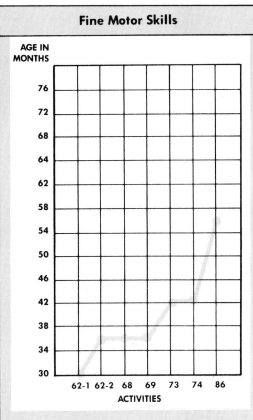

Fine Motor Skills

9
BEYOND THE PROGRAM

After completing the Gerard Method, youngsters will have mastered all the basic motor skills. When they are on their own, whether hanging on the jungle gym, climbing a tree, jumping rope or playing kickball, they will handle themselves safely and competently.

So what is the next step? There is no need for a maintenance program, because the skills that have been mastered will be drawn on for the rest of your child's life. Kids are naturally active, a constant challenge to parents who want to provide creative outlets for their energy. Even after your child has finished the program, you can combine learned activities in new ways, to create games and exercises that are stimulating as well as fun. Especially on days when playing outdoors is impossible, this is a great way to let your youngster burn up excess energy without getting out of hand.

Undoubtedly, the child who feels confident and comfortable when engaged in physical activities will have a natural interest in pursuing them. So while I do not believe that school-age youngsters should necessarily pursue a more formal program for sports or dance training, this is one way parents can help their children get hooked on the exercise habit.

For interested youngsters, this chapter offers practical tips on choosing a sport and joining organized programs. Young graduates of the Gerard Method program have a broad base of movement experience, giving them a head start over many of their peers who are beginning the same activity or sport. Still, a bad experience with an unqualified teacher or in a sport ill matched to his skills can turn off a youngster to physical endeavors for life. Here are some guidelines to ensure a continuing positive learning experience for the child who has an interest in movement and athletics.

• First of all, it's important to select the class or athletic club best suited to your child's abilities. As his "personal coach" for the past six years, you are in a unique position to know the skill areas in which he excels. If you have been filling out the evaluation graphs during the program, simply look them over to identify the areas of strength and weakness. Consider your child to be strong in those skill areas where his individual graph is on a par with or better than average overall, and weak where it is below average. Excluding balance, determine the one skill area in which your child most excels.

• From the chart below, choose one or two activities that

complement as well as challenge your child's natural abilities. This chart groups activities according to skill requirements. You'll notice that good balance, which is the foundation of all movement, is an integral part of each category.

STRENGTH BALANCE	gymnastics	wrestling
	ballet	synchronized swimming
COORDINATION BALANCE	gymnastics	fencing
	ballet	volleyball
	tap dance	baseball
	rhythmic gymnastics	basketball
		soccer
	skiing	ice hockey
	diving	field hockey
	judo	softball
	tennis	table tennis
GROSS MOTOR BALANCE	track and field	swimming
	ice skating	rowing
	roller skating	cycling
	skiing	
FINE MOTOR BALANCE	violin	art classes
	piano	craft classes

• Once you have selected a skill suited to your child's talents, locate the programs or schools in your area that provide introductory classes for children in the activity. But before you enroll your youngster in any class:
– Call the school and ask about the teacher's credentials and about the student-teacher ratio. Preferably, the teacher should have a degree in education and/or extensive experience working in the sport or the field of art or music as well as working with young children. Ideally, there should be only six to eight students—and never more than twelve—per instructor.

– With your youngster, visit a class in session. Determine if the instructor seems to have a good rapport with children. The classroom environment should be safe, upbeat and fun. Remember, for a first introduction to an activity, your child needs a great teacher, not a world-class performer. If possible, have the teacher meet your child.
• Sign up your child in the class or program that most satisfies his needs. If your child expresses a strong interest in taking classes, enroll him for a limited time to start—preferably not more than six weeks—so your financial commitment is minimal. Before he begins, discuss the class with him. Let him know that you are very excited about it, too, and that you believe he will enjoy it very much. However, if your child loses interest before the six weeks are up, or if he doesn't like the teacher, don't force him to complete the classes. At the end of the trial period, let your child decide for himself if he would like to continue.

The Gerard Method does not advocate pushing children at any age, either to learn physical activities or to do them. You have already invested great time and care in the program to give your child a sound foundation and appreciation of physical activity, so don't risk a negative social and psychological experience now by pressuring him into training or study if he doesn't want to be there.

Movement and sports provide valuable opportunities in life for self-expression, social interaction and positive challenge. Most of all, they can provide hour after hour of fun. Whether youngsters become involved in athletics or prefer to play tag and Frisbee with friends, they will enjoy the unique physical and inner resources this program has given them for years to come.

ACTIVITY INDEX